T0355602

ISABEL "LEFTY" ALVAREZ

Isabel "Lefty" Alvarez

The Improbable Life of a Cuban American Baseball Star

Kat D. Williams

UNIVERSITY OF NEBRASKA PRESS   LINCOLN

Portions of this book were previously published in
*The All-American Girls after the AAGPBL: How Playing
Pro Ball Shaped Their Lives* © 2017 Kat D. Williams by
permission of McFarland & Company, Inc., Box 611,
Jefferson NC 28640. www.mcfarlandbooks.com.

Unless otherwise noted, photos are from Isabel
"Lefty" Alvarez's personal collection.

Library of Congress Cataloging-in-Publication Data
Names: Williams, Kat D., author.
Title: Isabel "Lefty" Alvarez: the improbable life of
a Cuban American baseball star / Kat D. Williams.
Description: Lincoln: University of Nebraska Press,
2020. | Includes bibliographical references and index.
Identifiers: LCCN 2019044424
ISBN 9781496218827 (hardback: alk. paper)
ISBN 9781496221650 (epub)
ISBN 9781496221667 (mobi)
ISBN 9781496221674 (pdf)
Subjects: LCSH: Alvarez, Isabel, 1933– | All-American
Girls Professional Baseball League—History. | Women
baseball players—United States—Biography. |
Women baseball players—Cuba—Biography.
Classification: LCC GV865.A46 W55 2020 |
DDC 796.357/8092 [B]—dc23
LC record available at https://lccn.loc.gov/2019044424

Set in Lyon by Mikala R. Kolander.
Designed by N. Putens.

For my mom, Sara Williams
1937–2018

CONTENTS

ILLUSTRATIONS

PREFACE

The story of Isabel "Lefty" Alvarez is one that can be told through various lenses. We could celebrate her athletic talent and her bravery. Her life as an immigrant could be the focus, or we could simply place her within the history of the All-American Girls Professional Baseball League (AAGPBL). Lefty's story is complicated and should be told from each of these perspectives. Lefty can be understood only if all aspects of her life and identity are examined. This biography seeks to do just that by employing a new category of analysis, which I call sport-identity, to tell Lefty's life story. Such an approach allows for a better understanding of her life, how and why she made the decisions she did, and the ways in which she relied on the identity she created to survive a difficult life. For many women, including Lefty, sport becomes the dominate element of their identity because it also provides a way to hide the things that make them feel inferior. If, as was true for Lefty, participating in sports becomes a refuge from the physical and emotional difficulties of school or family, it becomes a replacement for those negative aspects of women's lives and takes over as the location where self-esteem, motivation, and confidence flourish, thereby becoming the most dominant element of their identities.

With the goal in mind of observing the role of sports in women's lives, this book looks beyond the synthesized Hollywood story of women in the AAGPBL to understand how the AAGPBL affected those who played in it. Specifically this biography delves into the life of professional baseball player Isabel "Lefty" Alvarez to analyze how the game changed the life of this fifteen-year-old Cuban immigrant forever. Tracing Lefty's life from her childhood in Cuba, where she played baseball with the boys on the streets of El Cerro (the neighborhood in Havana in which she grew up), to the life she established after the league ended, Lefty's story is interesting and worth telling for many reasons. Her immigration from Cuba makes this a story about a Latina following the baseball dream to America, and her lifelong devotion to the AAGPBL gives us a different look into the story of the league as well.

The intersection of Lefty's baseball experience, her nationality, gender, class, and sexuality represents for Lefty the sum of her identity. She is not only female, working class, Cuban American, or a former baseball player; rather she is the sum of all those parts. No one, regardless of his or her athletic ability or connection to sports, is defined by one dimension, of course. But for women who are sport-identified, and particularly lesbians, sport is not just a profession or a hobby; it does not simply make them more physically fit or more self-confident. It is also the place, the intersection, where all other identity markers (race, class, sexuality) converge to create gender identity.

ACKNOWLEDGMENTS

This book exists because Maybelle Blair called me out of the blue one day and said, "Kat, you need to write this book." She knew that Lefty's story was important and believed I should be the one to tell it. On more than one occasion she brought both Lefty and me to her home in California so that we would have uninterrupted days to talk face to face. She facilitated numerous other interviews, and for ten years Blair encouraged, nudged, and finally demanded I get it done. I did—and in large part thanks to her.

From its inception this project benefited from the help and support of numerous other friends and family. They always encouraged: "Write the damn book!" Eventually I did, mostly because they always thought I could. My mom and dad, T. J. and Sara Williams, taught me to love baseball, and it was that early connection to the game that set me on this path. It was their never-ending love and support that kept me on it. I only wish my mom was here to see this book in print. My sister, Kim Williams, always believed in me, provided encouragement, and never ceased to show pride in what I do. The sheer force of her spirit keeps me afloat.

Greta Rensenbrink, my spouse, my friend, and my soul mate, made this book possible in so many ways. From reading drafts, to editing, to taking over household chores, to dog walking, to countless pep talks, she gave the love and support crucial to this book. Without her I would still be sitting in my chair saying, "Blair thinks I should write this book."

To my Rensenbrink/Karczewski family members, who always support me in everything I do, thank you is simply not enough. As with all things, writing this book was so much easier with all of you on my side.

Along this path I made great friends but none greater than Donna Cohen. By sheer happenstance we became partners, friends, and determined advocates for women's baseball and for each other. Thankfully for every Mule there is a Nag, and during the completion of this book I relied on her ability to be both. Thank you, my friend.

My extended baseball family, the team that makes up the International Women's Baseball Center—Perry Barber, Maybelle Blair, Shirley Burkovich, Donna Cohen, Leslie Heaphy, Cami Kidder, Debbie Pierson, Greg Schwanke, and Ryan Woodward—made this journey much easier. Thank you for the support and especially the friendship.

Finally and most important, thank you to Isabel "Lefty" Alvarez. From the first time I met Lefty, I knew she was special, a treasure. First, she became my friend. Then she became the subject of a ten-year project. Along the way I got to know her better, and with every story she told me, I loved and respected her more. Thank you for the example you set and for giving me the privilege of telling your story. Here's to you, the rascal of El Cerro.

Unless otherwise noted, all quotations are from recorded interviews that are in my possession. My initial interview with Lefty took place in Grand Rapids, Michigan, on June 8, 2007, and subsequent interviews were conducted in Palm Springs, California, on February 16, 2009; October 11, 2009; June 6 and 11, 2011; and via telephone on October 20, 2011. I interviewed Lefty with Nancy Blee in Palm Springs, California in February 2011. I interviewed Annabelle Lee Harmon in Palm Springs in 2006. I interviewed Maybelle Blair in Palm Springs on January 24, 2008, and July 23, 2011, and in Orlando, Florida, on June 2 and 3, 2015. I interviewed Shirley Burkovich in Palm Springs on January 23, 2008, and in Orlando on June 2 and 3, 2015. I had telephone interviews with Terry Donahue on June 10, 2007, and September 14, 2008. I interviewed Katie Horstman in Palm Springs on January 25, 2008; Karen Kunkel in Syracuse, New York, on September 12, 2003; and Jane Moffet, in Cape May, New Jersey, on May 9, 2006.

Throughout this book I will use "Lefty" rather than her first or last names. That is Lefty's request. She thinks that nickname, given to her by her teammates in the AAGPBL is a better representation of her than either of her other names.

INTRODUCTION

They called me the rascal. I was the little rascal of El Cerro.

ISABEL "LEFTY" ALVAREZ

In 2003 I attended my first reunion of the All-American Girls Professional Baseball League Players Association (AAGPBL). It remains one of my most treasured memories, in part because that was also the first time I met Isabel "Lefty" Alvarez. One of my earliest memories of Lefty is in a crowded hotel restaurant. As I stood waiting to be seated, a group of women arrived (I learned later they were former players of the AAGPBL) and began asking everyone who passed if they had seen Lefty. No one had, and it seemed they were concerned that Lefty had not returned from the day's events. "I knew she would get lost," one woman said. "She is stubborn," replied another. "I don't know how she ever gets where she is going," added a third.

I was seated and lost track of where the group had gone until a rousing cheer went up from the back of the restaurant as a short, bubbly woman rushed in claiming, "Holy cow! I got lost again. This place is confusing for a little Cuban like me." Everyone laughed and teased her about getting lost, but the genuine relief that Lefty had returned safely was clear.

Sometime later I reminded Lefty of that story. She shook her head and said, "Well, I get lost a lot, but someone always finds me." The AAGPBL found Lefty in Havana, Cuba, in 1947. It is my hope that others will find her and her story as a result of this book. Her life should never be lost to us. Lefty's story is relevant to the world of baseball, to Cuban and American history, and especially to the long and mostly unmined history of women's baseball.[1]

Lefty's life was largely shaped by what Cubans themselves refer to as the "passion of the island": baseball. When it comes to sports, the love of and connection to baseball transcend all age groups and genders.[2] Baseball has long been important to the fabric of Cuban society, and in fact the game's popularity was so widespread in the late nineteenth century that the Spanish, fearing Cubans would distance themselves from European sports such as bull fighting, banned the game. This act inadvertently made the game a symbol of Cuban freedom and independence, thus further enhancing its popularity. Through the fight for Cuban independence from Spain in 1898, through the county's economic woes during the world economic depression of the 1930s, and even through the Cuban Revolution under Fidel Castro, baseball was a constant for Cubans and provided a comforting presence for Cubans of all classes and genders. From its earliest days on the island, baseball was connected to the core of Cuba and of Cubans.

To Lefty baseball provided a safe haven away from the economic, political, and familial struggles that filled her world. Lefty does not remember a time when her country or her family was not in some stage of turmoil. "[From] what I understand we have always been fighting for something in my country," she said. She learned to ignore many of the political and economic challenges of her country, which were many during her early life. She was born into a worldwide economic depression and in the midst of political upheaval in Cuba. Her parents struggled to handle both while raising a family, but unfortunately many of the outside world's woes flooded into their home. "Thank God I had a sport self that helped me in those times. I think maybe we all find ways to be okay, but me? I find my sport self." From an early age Lefty watched as her mother, a dedicated baseball fan, listened to games on the radio in their El Cerro house, just blocks from the Gran Stadium, where the Almendares and the Cienfuegos baseball teams played and where, later, the New York Yankees and the women of the AAGPBL would play exhibition games. Along with many other children Lefty and her brother played baseball with homemade balls on the streets of their neighborhood. She remembered those times fondly. "I was good at all sports," she said, "but it was baseball that made me and my mother the happiest." Baseball, more than any other sport, gave Lefty solace, but as she realized later in life, it was also baseball that most connected her to a proud Cuban heritage.

The history of Cuba is rich with baseball, music, food, and art. But it is also a history full of class struggles, American intervention, and revolution. In the years before the Cuban Revolution in the 1950s the country suffered at the hands of brutal leaders and outside forces, and after the revolution the country fought to create a strong, independent government that represented all Cubans. Over the next four decades the country also struggled economically, and despite a number of attempts to reform the economy, many Cubans lived in poverty, with few work or educational opportunities. These class struggles created the backdrop for Lefty's life and the lives of her parents.

Lefty's father, an orphan, was born into one Cuban revolution and came of age in another. Adopted by a Catholic priest and raised in relative wealth, he still struggled during the country's economic and political woes. Lefty's mother grew up in poverty and suffered daily as a result of Cuba's continued economic unrest. "My parents had a hard time, especially my mother," Lefty said. "That is why she wanted me to leave and never come back. It was a hard life for girls there. She wanted more for me, so when I was a kid, all I did was play, play sports, all sports. [Playing sports] kind of hid me from all [the troubles]. But I knew." Despite her mother's best efforts Lefty absorbed much of what was happening around her and was eventually able to weave together the stories of revolution and the lives of her parents. The result is an amazing tale of survival, patriotism, and political as well as personal revolution. It is in that historical, political, and baseball-related context that Isabel María Lucila Álvarez de León y Cerdán was born on October 31, 1933.

As noted above, this biography of Lefty fits into many familiar historical narratives: a Cuban American who proves herself through success on the playing field, a feminist hero, a woman who triumphs in a male-dominated world, an impoverished immigrant who makes good through hard work and determination. None of these stories, however, limited as they are to the traditional lenses of race, gender, and class, provides us with an image of Lefty that she would recognize. In order to more fully recognize Lefty, sport must be included in the discussion—and not just as her profession or hobby but as a crucial part of her identity. With the new category of analysis, sport-identity, a more complete picture of Lefty will emerge. Sport-identity is not a category that has historically been used in social movements and is not one that women have applied to themselves. But when I talk about such a category with athletically inclined women, there is an immediate recognition. They get it intuitively, without many words needing to be spoken. This is the "Aha!" moment, the shock of recognition, that feminists in the 1970s used to describe a moment of feminist awakening. This moment is the foundation of my assertion that sport-identity is an identity category and can be a category of analysis offering a new approach to our thinking about the many intersections and layers that make up identity.

The idea of sport-identity came about in part because I was trying to take the advice of Susan Cahn, who argues in her book *Coming on Strong* that historians of women's sports need to move beyond a simple retelling of female athletes' stories or the "See: women were here too" kinds of stories. Rather, she has argued, we need to find ways to use sports and women's role in sports to complicate things, not simplify them. Using sports as a tool allows us to generate new histories about race, class, sexuality, or other categories of identity important to an understanding of the connection between sport and gender. Cahn's own use of oral histories and her probing gender and class analyses allow her to examine tensions between the supposed "masculine" world of sports and the participation of female athletes.[3] Applying sport-identity to Lefty's biography allows for just the kind of rethinking that Cahn calls for.

Sport-identity can be understood as an identity category that works very much in the way that race, class, gender, and sexuality do in defining and shaping identity. As such it should be applied in the same way as these other categories of analysis. Like those more traditional categories, sport-identity is based on lived experience and can be understood as an expression of the self. While playing sports allows even weekend athletes to feel whole, confident, and more fully and comfortably in their bodies, for the sport-identified, sport is at their very core. Women experience sport-identity in various ways. For some it is physical. There is a sense of physical confidence that a woman can feel in the way she moves and walks, a muscle memory that shapes responses even far from the playing field in space and time. She can feel it in herself and recognize it in others. Others experience it emotionally, as sport creates an affirmation of self. Most powerfully it can be a way of expressing something that feels most true about oneself. When I asked friends whom I consider sport-identified to reflect on their childhoods and the role sports played in their lives, most answered with something like, "I didn't feel like myself when I wasn't playing." Or, "I didn't even know who I was, like if I looked in a mirror, I would not see me, not the real me." If we fail to recognize the significance of such expressions for women like Lefty, we begin to lose sight of them as well.

Few women are more sport-identified than Lefty Alvarez. This identity is apparent in Lefty's claim that sport informs her, "ties the other parts of me together." In that moment it is the location where all layers of her identity intersect. This biography explores the major events of Lefty's life through the lens of sport. It does not attempt to elevate her status in the game of baseball or to make her a Cuban hero. Rather it seeks to show how one woman used sport to survive. Lefty relied on what she herself calls her "sport self" to survive a life filled with personal insecurities, the struggles of immigration, the difficulties of being a young woman alone in a country where she did not speak the language or understand the customs, and the loss of the one thread that held her together, the AAGPBL. From her early life in Cuba through old age, Lefty needed and always used the part of her identity that was informed by sport, and we cannot understand her story without acknowledging that identity marker. By using sport-identity, it is possible to demonstrate how sport can and does alter, shape, and maintain the identity of Lefty Alvarez.

Chapter One, "El Cerro," provides context for Lefty's life by explaining the Cuban world of revolution and reform, and the political and economic hardships of her family, in which she and her brother grew up. Chapter Two, "Refashioning Lefty," focuses on Lefty's family relationships and specifically on her mother's challenging expectations. It was during this time that sport became so crucial to Lefty's survival. Whether it was in a classroom, at home while trying to live up to her mother's dreams, or on the streets of Havana, a young Isabel relied on sport to carry her through difficult times.

Chapter Three, "The Passion of the Island," explores the history and significance of baseball to all aspects of Cuban life and culture. It also begins to explain the impact baseball had on Lefty, how she embraced that history and used it. Finally, it places Lefty within the context of that history by showing her role in it. Chapter Four, "Coming to America," further illustrates Lefty's role in baseball history by examining her move from Cuba to the United States. A focus on Lefty's years in the AAGPBL highlights how her connection to sport, especially baseball, helped her survive loneliness, learning a new language, difficult relationships, and ultimately alcohol abuse. The centrality of sport to Lefty's life after her professional career ended is the focus of Chapter Five, "My Life after the League." Sport remained an important part of her identity, but the ways in which she used it and the reasons for using it changed over time. Chapter Six, "A League of Her Own," demonstrates the lifelong effects of the AAGPBL on Lefty and the others who played in the league. The chapter begins with the 1980s, when the AAGPBL players' association was established and explores the thrill of the league's first being recognized by the National Baseball Hall of Fame in Cooperstown and finally by the world after the release of the movie *A League of Their Own* in 1992. Chapter Seven examines what Lefty's true legacy is to women's baseball, Cuban immigration, and American women's history. Because Lefty herself acknowledges that "No matter which slice of my life you look at, it is nothing until it is touched by sport," this chapter also discusses Lefty as an example of sport-identity. There are two appendices in the book. The first shows Lefty's professional statistics, which she rarely mentioned but which I thought should be included. Because she was and is very much a part of both American and Cuban baseball history, the second appendix is a time line of women's baseball history. Lefty asked very little of me as I worked on this project, but in one of our last conversations she made me promise to show in "one of those long lists in the back of books," the rich history of Cuban sports. She has always been a proud Cuban American and wanted the world to know that she is simply the product of good "sporting stock."

ISABEL "LEFTY" ALVAREZ

CHAPTER ONE

El Cerro

My mother loved baseball and America. And since she couldn't play baseball or go to America, from my beginning she planned my life in both.

LEFTY ALVAREZ

"Our history is one of problems," Isabel "Lefty" Alvarez says about Cuba. "I don't understand most of our history, but I know about a lot of it because my father was a friend and supporter of Batista." When Lefty was born in Havana, Fulgencio Batista y Zaldívar was Cuba's president, dictator, and military leader. Lefty's father became a policeman in Batista's regime in 1933. Resistance to Batista's rule soon took its place in Cuba's century-long struggle for independence and self-determination. Ultimately Lefty's family would split painfully over these issues.

As a country Cuba survived those struggles, and Lefty's parents did the same. In the end Lefty believes that part of her ability to survive difficult times comes from being Cuban and living in a country that struggled, survived, thrived, and then struggled again as it fought against dictators and outside influence. The hard-fought victories that resulted made their mark on Lefty. "I may not always know how to do it at first, but I always figure out how to win—you know, come out on top. Guess it is either stubbornness or my Cubanness," Lefty explains with a laugh. It is likely some of both. As Lefty says, Cuban history is one of upheaval and conflict, but it is also a history of perseverance, resistance, and revolution. At times Lefty needed the lessons she learned from the determination of her countrymen. "Being from fighters, I guess I was a fighter too," she remarks.

Cuba's long history of determination started in the nineteenth century with the country's fight for independence. In the sixteenth century the Spanish colonized Cuba. Looking for wealth, they realized that the fertile ground of Cuba was ripe for growing tobacco, which soon became the country's primary export. The tobacco trade was very lucrative for the Spanish, and in order to provide more labor, they brought African slaves to the island. Due in part to the island's tobacco production and later its production of sugarcane, colonial powers fought over the control of Cuba. During the Seven Years' War, a conflict fought between 1756 and 1763 that involved every European power of the time and spanned five continents, the British conquered the port of Havana and introduced thousands more slaves into Cuba. The Haitian Revolution, which took place in nearby Saint-Domingue (a French colony in the western part of Haiti) from 1791 to 1804, resulted in thousands of French refugees arriving in Cuba. They brought with them more slaves and an expertise in sugar refining and coffee growing, both of which required a lot of field labor. These events created an ethnically and economically diverse population in Cuba and set the stage for future Cuban battles over racial and economic disparities.

With more diversity came widespread inequality among the races and eventually rebellion. The economic growth Cuba enjoyed as a result of the tobacco and sugar exports brought with it a wave of bourgeois reformism. Cuban plantation owners such as Francisco de Agüero y Parreno, one of the first and most influential reform leaders, led economic reform efforts that would secure benefits for the slave-owning sector of society. They were very successful. Believing that the growth of Cuba's economy was tied not to the workers but to the plantation class, the government supported efforts to strengthen the owners' hold on the land and the slaves who worked it. It did not take long, however, before the independence movements of South America and word of the region's independence from Spain spread to Cuba. That knowledge, along with a growing nationalist sentiment, spelled the end of bourgeois reform and marked the beginning of social reformism.[1]

One of the country's first and perhaps most influential leaders of social reform was José Antonio Saco, a proponent of Cuban nationalism and an outspoken critic of the Spanish. He was popular among the young intellectuals, and his teachings were in direct opposition to those of the bourgeoisie. Saco was the editor of the magazine *Revista Bimestre Cubana* and a favorite writer among younger Cubans unhappy with the current plantation system.

He argued that the arrival of large numbers of slaves from Africa would lead to revolution because, he felt, the black race was not to be trusted. While Saco's opposition to the slave trade was not based on humanitarian concerns, it did bring to the forefront the many problems with colonialism. He argued that the Spanish government supported the slave trade in Cuba because it meant Cuba would have to rely on the Spanish military for protection, thereby making the country more reliant on Spain. The plantation class and the colonial government wanted Saco out of Cuba, so he was exiled in 1834.[2] The struggle to end slavery in Cuba was long and bitter. The plantation system was weakened as a result, but eventually bourgeois reformist ideas reemerged. It was from the remnants of both reform movements that a growing independence movement emerged.

Cuba's fight for independence was long and painful. In 1868 the first of the independence wars began. The Ten Years' War, also known as the Great War, lasted until 1878. This early push for independence was led by Cuban-born planters and other wealthy natives not linked to the colonial plantation system. On October 10, 1868, sugar mill owner Carlos Manuel de Céspedes and his followers began an uprising that spread very rapidly.[3] In April 1869 followers of Céspedes drew up a constitution that established the Republic of Cuba; then they set up a three-pronged form of government that included an executive, legislative, and judicial branch. With a new government and a new constitution established, the revolutionaries proclaimed independence from Spain. Céspedes was elected president of the republic.

The primary goals of the new republic were to achieve national independence from Spain and to abolish slavery.[4] Neither goal was easy to accomplish. Officially slavery had been abolished in the constitution of 1869, but in reality it still existed well into 1870. As the Ten Years' War continued, black and white rebels fought side by side across the country. Serving as models, the racially integrated rebel groups helped to move the country toward national integration.[5] The path to freedom from Spanish rule was long and most definitely did not end with the conclusion of the Ten Years' War. By 1871 branches of the newly formed government were at odds, and General Máximo Gómez, the military commander of the war for independence, had moved his troops westward in an attempt to bring the revolution to the whole country. Early in 1875 Gómez, with fewer than two thousand men, moved further westward into the Spanish strongholds from Júcaro to Morón.[6] The troops burned sugar mills and farms along the way and freed any slaves they encountered. It seemed that the colonial power in Cuba was finally crumbling. The troops were unable to convince regional forces to join Gómez's push westward. Instead officers asked Gómez to step down and sought the appointment of Aresenio Martínez Campos.[7] The rebels were fractured, and that lack of unity combined with a lack of support from abroad all but insured their defeat. On February 10, 1878, the Ten Years' War came to an end with the signing of the Pact of Zanjón.[8] Despite ten years of fighting, Cuba did not secure independence from Spain and failed to create an independent government or a nation-state. It did, however, gain a great deal of political and military experience, both of which were useful in subsequent attempts at independence.

Two other wars for independence followed in quick succession. The Little War lasted only one year, from 1879 to 1880, and was in many ways a continuation of the Ten Years' War. It had some of the same origins and same leaders. Following his release from prison after the Pact of Zanjón Pact, Cuban rebel Calixto García organized the Cuban Revolutionary Committee with other revolutionaries. In 1878 he issued a manifesto against the Spanish rule of Cuba. This met with approval among other revolutionary leaders, and war began on August 26, 1879.[9] Having been one of the few revolutionaries who did not sign the Pact of Zanjón, Calixto García led the revolution. From the beginning the revolutionaries faced many problems. They lacked experienced leaders, and they had a shortage of weapons and ammunition. They had no foreign allies, the population was exhausted from the Ten Years' War, and most people sought peace.[10] By September 1880 the rebels had been completely defeated.

Even though rebels had attempted to push for independence in the Little War, more Cubans were focused on what became known as the "Rewarding Truce." This truce, between the colonial government and the rebels, lasted for seventeen years, from the end of the Ten Years' War in 1878 until 1895. During those years there were fundamental changes in Cuban society. With the abolition of slavery in October 1886, newly freed slaves became farmers and members of the urban working class.[11] Yet the economy could not sustain itself with all the changes, and as a result many wealthy Cubans lost their property. The number of sugar mills dropped, and inefficiency increased. Only large companies and the most powerful plantation owners remained in business.[12] These failures encouraged a new wave of revolutionary sentiment. While in exile for challenging the Spanish government in his new paper, *La Patria Libre*, José Martí mobilized the support of the Cuban exile communities in Florida, especially Key West. His goal was to lead a revolution that would achieve independence from Spain. In addition to rallying Cuban exiles, Martí also lobbied against U.S. plans to annex Cuba, a move desired by some politicians in both the United States and Cuba.

U.S. secretary of state James G. Blaine's plan to annex Cuba was well documented. Blaine wrote the following in early 1881: "That rich island, the key to the Gulf of Mexico, is, though in the hands of Spain, a part of the American commercial system. . . . If ever ceasing to be Spanish, Cuba must necessarily become American and not fall under any other European domination"[13] Martí was not deterred by increasing U.S. threats to annex. In December 1894 three ships (the *Lagonda*, the *Almadis*, and the *Baracoa*), loaded with weapons and Cuban revolutionaries, set sail for Cuba from Fernandina Beach, Florida. Two of the ships were seized by U.S. authorities in early January 1895, but the third ship made it to Cuba. Determined, Martí wrote what would become the official document of the Revolutionary Party in Cuba, the Manifesto of Montecristi. The document, signed by Martí and Máximo Gómez, outlined the reasons that Cuba fought to become an independent country. The manifesto also declared that the war would be fought by segregated forces, urging Afro-Cubans and whites alike to take up arms. In addition, any Spaniards who did not object to the war would be spared. It also stated that private rural properties should not be damaged and that the revolution should bring new economic life to Cuba.[14]

The Martí-led revolution began on February 24, 1895, with uprisings all over the island. In early April 1895 many of the revolution's main leaders landed in Oriente. Major General Antonio Maceo arrived with twenty-two leaders near Baracoa, and José Martí, Máximo Gómez, and four others arrived in Playitas.[15] Around that time Spanish forces in Cuba numbered approximately eighty thousand. Twenty thousand of them were regular troops, full-time members of the military, and the remaining sixty thousand were Spanish and Cuban volunteer militia.[16] The volunteer militia, along with slaves "volunteered" by wealthy land owners, was responsible for policing duties on the island, leaving the regular troops to defend against the rebels. By December, Spain had increased its troops in Cuba to nearly one hundred thousand, and the colonial government had increased the volunteer corps to sixty-three thousand. By the end of 1897 Spanish forces in Cuba numbered approximately three hundred thousand.[17]

The revolutionaries were outnumbered, but they were not without determination or dedication. The decades of inequality Cubans had endured at the hands of Spanish and U.S. rule had made revolutionaries out of many Cubans and instilled in them a desire for freedom and independence. Cubans who lived in intense poverty in the countryside were among some of the most dedicated revolutionaries. Many suffered greatly during and even after the Ten Years' War. Sugar production was seasonal, and the *macheteros*, sugarcane cutters who worked only four months out of the year, were often unemployed and therefore barely managed to survive. Poor peasants were often seriously malnourished, and neither health care nor education was accessible to rural Cubans who lived in poverty. Illiteracy was widespread, and those lucky enough to attend school seldom made it past the first or second grades.[18] Such conditions helped fuel the Cuban revolutionaries' fight for independence.

Neither Spain nor the United States was going to release their economic and politic holds on Cuba without a fight, however. The war for Cuban independence lasted until 1898 and included many victories and numerous defeats for the Cuban rebels. For much of the war American U.S. involvement did not include direct military action. On February 15, 1898, that changed. On that day the battleship USS *Maine* exploded, killing 258 of the crew and sinking in the Havana harbor. At the time, a military board of investigations decided that the *Maine* had exploded due to the detonation of a mine underneath the hull. However, later investigations found that it was likely something inside the ship that had caused the explosion. The cause was of little concern to U.S. journalists, who seized on the explosion to push for U.S. involvement in the war for Cuban independence.

The sinking of the USS *Maine* sparked a wave of public outcry in the United States. Newspaper owners such as William R. Hearst leaped to the conclusion that Spanish officials in Cuba were to blame, and they widely publicized a conspiracy. Yellow journalism fueled U.S. anger by publishing "atrocities" committed by Spain in Cuba. Hearst, when informed by Frederic Remington (whom he had hired to furnish illustrations for his newspaper) that conditions in Cuba were not bad enough to warrant hostilities, allegedly replied, "You furnish the pictures and I'll furnish the war."[19] President William McKinley and much of the business community opposed the growing demand for war. But journalists continued to fan the flames by creating such rallying cries as, "Remember the *Maine*, to Hell with Spain!"

President McKinley could not hold back the pro-war push, so on April 11 he asked Congress for authority to send U.S. troops to Cuba for the purpose of ending the civil war. On April 19 Congress passed a joint resolution supporting Cuban independence and disclaiming any intention to annex Cuba.[20] The resolution demanded Spanish withdrawal from Cuba and authorized the president to use as much military force as he deemed necessary to help Cuba gain independence from Spain. The resolution included the Teller Amendment. The amendment declared that the United States would not exercise control over Cuba for any reason other than pacification and specified that U.S. forces would be removed once the civil war was over. President McKinley signed the resolution on April 2, 1898, and an ultimatum was sent to Spain. Spain responded by severing diplomatic relations with the United States; on the same day that the resolution was signed, the U.S. Navy began a blockade of Cuba. Spain threatened to declare war on the United States if it invaded Spanish territory. On April 20, 1898, the U.S. Congress formerly declared war against Spain, and thus began the War for Cuban Independence.[21]

Upon the declaration of war, the U.S. Navy quickly set up blockades at several Cuban ports, and within days U.S. ground troops landed in the country. The war's largest fight, a naval battle, took place at the port of Santiago on July 3, 1898. The battle resulted in the destruction of the Spanish Caribbean Squadron (Flota de Ultramar), an outcome that severely weakened the Spanish efforts in Cuba.[22] The superior strength of the U.S.

Navy, along with the large number of ground troops, left little doubt that the American forces would defeat the Spanish in Cuba. The United States widened its efforts against Spain, however, and fought the Spanish on many fronts, including the Philippines, Guam, and Puerto Rico. On May 1 American forces destroyed the Spanish fleet at Manila, and the United States began its invasion of the Philippines. U.S. invasions of Guam and Puerto Rico soon followed.

On December 10, 1898, the Treaty of Paris, which ended the war, was signed by the United States and Spain. The United States took credit for helping to liberate Cuba and in the process managed to acquire Puerto Rico, Guam, and the Philippines as colonies for itself. In 1901 the United States insisted that the Cubans include the Platt Amendment in their newly written constitution.[23] The amendment gave the United States a military base on the island (Guantanamo) and allowed for future intervention into Cuba if U.S. military or economic interests were over in jeopardy.

U.S. occupation officially lasted from 1898 until 1902. During that time and even into the early years of the republic the United States controlled much of the Cuban economy, especially the sugar industry. As early as 1899 the United States began acquiring many of the sugar estates. Companies such as the American Sugar Company and the United Fruit Company purchased tens of thousands of acres. In addition, U.S. real estate companies acquired titles to large tracts of land; by 1905 close to thirteen thousand Americans from the United States had purchased land in Cuba, and an estimated 60 percent of all rural property in Cuba was owned by individuals or corporations from the United States.[24] In addition to land, U.S. and Spanish companies bought Cuba railroads, mines, banks, and cigar factories. Foreign control over the Cuban economy ensured that the gap between the rural and urban populations would continue and that the poor of the country would remain both poor and, now, landless. The war for Cuban independence brought independence from Spain, but it also brought a country to economic, social, and physical ruin.

The prewar Cuban population was 1.8 million, but at the war's end the population had dropped to just under one million.[25] The scars of war were visible everywhere. Houses, roads, bridges, and railroads had been destroyed.

Commerce was at a standstill, manufacturing was halted, and mines were closed. Regardless of size, towns and villages had been reduced to rubble.[26] Many Cubans, especially those from the impoverished countryside, began to question why they had fought a war for independence since life for them had only gotten worse. Cuba began nationhood with its social order and its class structure in total disarray.

Many Cubans lost personal fortunes and private property to bring independence to Cuba. Property and business owners, along with wage earners and peasants, were expelled from the land where they had worked and lived, and everywhere Cubans faced a decline in employment opportunities. None struggled more than Afro-Cubans. Their lives did not improve after the final war for Cuban independence; in fact they became much more difficult for many. As Martí had asked them to do, Afro-Cubans had fought for Cuban independence alongside their white countrymen, and they too had believed in the hope of independence and all it promised to Cubans. Unfortunately, however, over 72 percent of Afro-Cubans were illiterate, so a large number did not meet the suffrage requirements spelled out in the 1901 constitution. These requirements meant that Afro-Cubans had very little voice in the newly formed government, and as a result they did not benefit from the revolution in the ways they had hoped. One former slave and revolutionary, Esteban Montejo, whose story was made famous in his book, *Biography of a Runaway Slave*, remarked, "After the war ended . . . the Negroes found themselves out in the streets—men brave as lions, out in the streets. It was unjust, but that's what happened. There wasn't even one percent of Negroes in the police force."[27] This widespread exclusion from government jobs, politics, and education widened the divide between whites and Cubans of color and continued to fan the flames of revolt. In spite of the war's official end in 1898 Afro-Cubans protested their treatment and especially their continued exclusion from the government and public offices long after peace was declared.

Despite the promises of liberation, social justice, better education, and freedom, neither Cubans of color nor women of all races benefitted from such promises. Like Afro-Cubans, in the years immediately after the war women in Cuba faced more, not fewer, limitations and challenges. Even before the war women had few political rights; unfortunately the 1901 constitution did little to elevate their status. Women were denied the right to vote in the new government, and there were no provisions to address the overall inequalities between men and women in Cuban society. This divide is most obvious in education and employment. Women did not have adequate educational opportunities; as a result, nearly 52 percent of all white women were illiterate in the years immediately after the war for independence. The numbers were much higher for women of color. Over 70 percent of Afro-Cuban women were illiterate. The lack of educational opportunities led to few employment options for women. In 1899 women made up 10.6 percent of the wage labor force; 63 percent of those women were listed as "domestic workers."[28] The low numbers do not reflect a lack of need for employment or even a lack of interest among workers. Rather, they demonstrate how few opportunities existed for women in postwar Cuba. With no voice in the government and few educational or employment opportunities, neither Afro-Cubans nor women of any race experienced positive changes after independence.

The continued discriminatory practices against such a large percentage of the population shaped Cuba's social, economic, and political reality in the immediate postwar period. In 1908 Cubans of color created the Partido Independiente de Color, which put together a full slate of candidates for public office. It was not successful, but it posed a threat to the ruling Liberal Party, which had been traditionally supported by blacks. The response of the Cuban government was the enactment of the Morúa law, which prohibited the creation of a political party along racial lines. Many Partido Independiente leaders were arrested, and in May 1912 the party resorted to armed rebellion. Thousands of Afro-Cubans were killed in the ensuing revolt. Even though the conflict was not successful in bringing immediate change for Cubans of color, it revealed to the government what would happen if it continued to ignore large portions of the population. Still corruption flourished in the government; despite the revolt by the Afro-Cubans, by the end of the 1910s much of the wealth that had been created was spent by the Cuban government on consumption and investments abroad, with very little of it invested in the lives of Cubans.[29]

During the subsequent administrations of José Miguel Gómez (1908–12) and Mario G. Menocal (1912–20) 372 indictments were brought against public officials; by 1923 the number had increased to 483.[30] These indictments did little to stop political corruption, and politics continued to control the economy and to determine who could and should benefit from it. Government control of the country's economic structure ensured that poor Cubans, Afro-Cubans, and most women would be excluded. Indeed most Cubans continued to lose ground politically and economically. Adding to Cuba's already poor economic situation, in the early 1920s the beginning of the worldwide economic depression came early to Cuba.

The price of sugar dropped, and all sectors of the economy suffered as a result. Sugar workers were the hardest hit by the economic downturn. By the late 1920s the impact of the economic depression had intensified in Cuba, and by the end of the decade millions of Cubans were unemployed and living in poverty. Sugar producers found themselves with surplus sugar and declining prices. As a result, wages were reduced, workers were laid off, and businesses failed at a rapid rate. At this time nearly one million people (out of a population of 3.9 million) were unemployed.[31] Making the situation even worse, the United States passed the Hawley-Smoot Tariff Act, which increased the taxes on Cuban sugar.[32] Workers and business owners alike called for government help, but President Gerardo Machado refused to give it.

Machado's inaction led to political and social upheaval. Labor organized; as a result, union membership expanded. In 1927 cigar workers united in the Federación Nacional de Torcedores. The organization united over thirty thousand workers from all six provinces.[33] In addition, electrical workers, sugar workers, and construction and railroad workers also organized. As workers became more desperate, armed clashes between the unions and Machado's military increased in number and intensity. Eventually Machado ordered his military to crack down on the unions, and at a May 1, 1930, celebration in Regla many protestors were killed or injured. Within twenty-four hours nearly all ranking union leaders were either in jail or in exile.[34] Throughout the summer and into the early fall of 1930 protests spread and became increasingly violent. In January 1931 Machado invoked an old law of public order that suspended the publication of newspapers and periodicals that had been critical of him. The editors were arrested, and the military took over the publications. The government eliminated opposition through arrests, torture, assassinations, and intimidation.

The Franklin Roosevelt administration reacted to the brutality of the Machado government by sending Assistant Secretary of State Sumner Welles to Cuba in 1933. Welles was charged with brokering a "friendly mediation" that would create an understanding between the Cuban government and the factions opposed to it.[35] He was told to negotiate an end to the crisis. Both sides hoped they would benefit from Welles's efforts. The Machado government hoped Welles would work to ensure that Machado served out his full term, while the opposition wanted Welles to help develop a plan that would remove Machado. Welles promised each side what it wanted to hear, allowing the United States to help clear the way for Machado's retirement by creating a constitutional basis for presidential succession.[36]

The negotiations also gave Welles and the United States a forum through which opposition groups could be brought into the discussion. Groups gained legitimacy in this way and became visible participants in a political solution to Cuba's problems. In essence this served as a recruiting process. However, if the goals of opposition groups were not compatible with U.S. interests, they were not invited to participate. Representatives from mainstream opposition groups such as unions and those of university professors, women's groups, teachers, and the leaders of the Liberal, Conservative, and Popular Parties joined the mediations, which began on July 1, 1920.[37] Machado denounced U.S. intervention in Cuban affairs and urged Cubans to defend their homeland from such aggression. Before any rebellion could occur, however, bus drivers in Havana went on strike. Their clashes with police sparked more strikes, and eventually Havana was paralyzed. In early August the unrest came to a head when violence between protestors and police left several dead and hundreds injured. The result was an opening allowing the U. S. government to threaten armed intervention if Machado did not step down. Using the strike's political nature as an example of Machado's ineffectiveness, Welles demanded that Machado resign or risk U.S. military action. Members of the government began defecting; by August 7 leaders from the

Liberal, Conservative, and Popular Parties had endorsed the U.S.-backed retirement of Machado. The military moved against him on August 12, and on that same day Machado left Cuba for the Bahamas.[38]

Welles helped to install Carlos Manuel de Céspedes as Cuba's new president. Céspedes had no party affiliation or political background at all and was touted as an inoffensive compromise candidate. But that also meant he had no mandate and very little following. Political turmoil continued after his inauguration when sugar workers, railroad workers, and tobacco workers all went on strike. The end of the Céspedes government came in September 1933, when a group of army officers and enlisted men met to discuss the grievances of the latter. The officers refused to listen to the enlisted men, and the men, led by Sergeant Fulgencio Batista, held their post until the officers agreed to hear their concerns. Anti-government civilians rallied around the troops, and the "Sergeants' Revolt," as the actions became known, began.[39] The participants did not initially seek the overthrow of Céspedes's government but simply better pay and housing. It was anti-government civilians who helped transform the revolt into a full-fledged military coup. Out of this coalition came a political manifesto that announced a provisional government and the establishment of a democracy. The new government coalition lasted only a week, but Sergeant Fulgencio Batista had entered the Cuban consciousness.

From the early nineteenth century to the 1930s Cuba had been at war against imperialists and at times against itself. Generations of Cubans grew up knowing only political and economic unrest. As Lefty herself acknowledges, Cuba's history, and by extension her own, "is one of problems." From his birth, Lefty's father, Prudencio Eusébio Álvarez de León Valdés, had lived with war and unrest as a backdrop. He was born in 1904, just as Cuba was trying to figure out how to be an independent country. As were many children in Cuba at that time, Prudencio was left at an orphanage. There is no information about his family or whether the country's political and economic struggles led to his being left there, but it was a common practice during periods of economic hardship for mothers to leave their newborn babies at local orphanages.

Since Prudencio's mother left him within days of his birth, the only home he ever knew was provided by the priests who ran the Catholic facility, La Casa de Beneficencia y Maternidad de La Habana. Known by most as "the Beneficencia," the orphanage was a landmark in Havana. It had opened its doors to unwanted, abandoned, and orphaned children in 1705, when Cuba was still a Spanish colony. It was home to thousands of children who were left in the institution's care either because of a parent's death or the parent's inability to care for them.[40] The Beneficencia acted as a home, a school, a church, and at times even a hospital for the children left there.

The orphanage was founded by Bishop Jerónimo Valdés y Sierra; as a tribute to him most male children who were cared for by the institution were registered with the surname Valdés. From the nineteenth century onward the Beneficencia operated out of a building in the heart of Old Havana, within sight of Malecón Boulevard and the city's harbor. It was staffed by both priests and nuns (the latter from the Order of the Sisters of Charity of St. Vincent DePaul) and administered by a board of patrons under the supervision of the Economic Society of Friends of the Nation, an old and well-respected nonprofit civic institution. The orphanage differed from others in that on the side of the building there was a device called the *torno*. This was a turnstile where a mother unable to care for a newborn child—often an unwed mother afraid of the social consequences of her status—could place an infant from outside the building.[41] She could then turn the mechanism so that the baby was moved safely inside, ringing a bell to alert the nuns of the new arrival. The *torno* kept the mother's identity secret.

It was this method that Prudencio's mother had used when she left him at the Beneficencia. According to Lefty, boys normally stayed in the orphanage until at least the age of seventeen, but Lefty's father was taken in by a priest, Antonio Álvarez de León, who removed him from the orphanage when Prudencio was twelve. Father de León gave Prudencio his last name and raised him as his own son. Little is known about Prudencio's childhood, but according to Lefty, the family did not quite understand the relationship between her father and the priest who raised him. When asked about this relationship, Lefty responds, "We just knew not to ask. There were rumors about them, but we just didn't know." These rumors were about a possible sexual relationship between Prudencio and the priest. Even after

Prudencio's marriage to Lefty's mother, rumors about his sexuality continued among neighbors, and the subject always embarrassed Lefty and caused great shame.

After Prudencio left the home of Father de León—Lefty believes this would have been when he was around eighteen or nineteen—he joined the Cuban military. If Lefty's estimations are correct, he would have joined around 1922, while Cuba was suffering from the worldwide economic depression. According to Lefty, it was during that military service that Prudencio met Fulgencio Batista y Zaldívar. Prudencio became a very dedicated follower of Batista and later relied on him for employment. Prudencio's career in the Cuban military put him in a respected position, one in which he made a good living. That service, along with some money left to him by Father de León, meant that Prudencio was able to live a solidly middle-class lifestyle. In a country where class status was very important, he represented success and a bright future.

Lefty's mother, María Virtudes Cerdán Fernández (known as Virtudes), grew up in Melena del Sur in a very poor family.[42] "My grandfather was a very mean man," Lefty recalls about Virtudes's father. "He tried to kill my grandmother once by throwing a large pair of scissors at her, and I am sure he abused my mother too." Lefty continues:

> He was an alcoholic and a very mean drunk. He had a very bad temper, even when he wasn't drinking but especially when he was. My mother used to tell me that he tried to kill my grandmother many times. He would take my mother off for days and did not tell anyone where he took her. . . . I don't know what he did with her, but I am sure he abused her. No one in my family ever talked about it. . . . My mother told me, "I [Virtudes] am like my father. Not the alcohol but the anger." She was right too. I think I was afraid of my mother. She was not mean to me, but I was afraid for her. Yes that is it. I was afraid *for* her.

Much of Virtudes's story is unknown to Lefty, but she knows enough to declare that her mother's single goal was to escape the poverty and the hardships of her birth family, to become a "respectable" person. Marrying Prudencio was a way out of that difficult life. "There was not love between them" Lefty claims, "but my mother wanted wealth, or at least [she wanted] people to think she was wealthy, and she did not care how she got it." Growing up with an alcoholic and abusive father made her quest for respectability through marriage to Prudencio understandable. It was certainly not uncommon for couples to marry out of financial need, and Virtudes was not alone in her use of marriage to escape a difficult life. As Virtudes's life showed, sometimes such a tactic worked, but other times the escape was only temporary.

In 1928 Virtudes met and married Prudencio. Lefty does not know where or how her parents met, but she is confident that it was her mother who pursued her father. "She wanted to be respected," she says, and "a handsome man in that military uniform would help [achieve that goal]." After the wedding the couple left almost immediately for an extended honeymoon on Gran Canaria, Spain, the original home of Father de León. Either unaware of or unconcerned about the brewing global economic crisis, Prudencio invested most of his inheritance in apartments located on the Spanish island. The U.S. stock market crash of October 1929 and the ensuing Great Depression had not yet swept the world when the couple decided to move to Gran Canaria, so it is likely that Prudencio simply did not realize what was about to happen. As a result of manufacturing and world trade, the U.S. economy flourished in the 1920s, but the depression led to sharp declines in both, and the ripple effect reached every part of the global economy. Like so many others, Prudencio was not able to make a profit with his investments. Prudencio, Virtudes, and their growing family headed back to Cuba. Their first child, Antonio (named after Father de León), had been born March 16, 1932, in Spain. Virtudes was pregnant with Lefty when they returned to Cuba.

Prudencio's inability to make a profit from his investments crushed Virtudes's dreams of wealth and respect. When the growing family, broke and discouraged, moved back to Cuba in 1932, the stage was set for what Lefty calls a lifetime of disappointment for Virtudes. The knowledge that her parents had not married for love made Lefty very sad. She does not blame her mother for wanting to escape her very painful life, but the fact that Virtudes's decision to marry Prudencio had saved her from poverty for only a short time seemed an even greater cruelty.

Once back in Cuba, the family continued to struggle financially, but as a devoted follower of Fulgencio Batista y Zaldívar, Prudencio turned to his old friend for help. Batista was the union leader of Cuba's soldiers; as noted above, in 1933 he led the "Sergeants' Revolt" that replaced the provisional government of Carlos Manuel de Céspedes. Initially a coalition composed of five members, one each from the anti-Machado movement, was created. However, within days the representative for the students and professors of the University of Havana, Ramón Grau, was made president, while Batista became the army chief of staff with the rank of colonel. He effectively controlled the presidency. During this period Batista violently suppressed several attempts to end his control. Grau was president for just over one hundred days before Batista forced him to resign in January 1934. He was replaced by Carlos Mendieta. Within five days the United States recognized Cuba's new government, which lasted eleven months. For the next decade Batista ran the country from the background, using presidents as his puppets. First came Mendieta (1934–35), then José A. Barnet (1935–36), then Miguel Mariano Gómez (1936), and finally Federico Laredo Brú (1936–40), who held the largely ceremonial position while Batista ran the country with an iron fist. Fulgencio Batista y Zaldívar was, for all intents and purposes, president, dictator, and military leader. It was in this context that Prudencio became a policeman in Batista's regime in 1933, the same year that Lefty was born.

Lefty never knew a time when her father wasn't either working for or openly supporting Batista. She has very little firsthand knowledge of Prudencio's time in the police force, but she remembers that he was "very dedicated to Batista, and I think he worked for him for fifteen years." Since Batista was in control, either behind the scenes or as president, for only eleven years during his first reign, Lefty's memory is likely off. She was quite young when Prudencio's stint with the police ended, so much of her information about that time comes from her brother, who was a year older. Lefty remembers Antonio retelling stories of what he considered more glorious days for the family: "Our father had a uniform and was very well respected, he told me. People listened to him, and that meant they respected us too." Lefty's brother was more impressed with his father than Lefty was. Lefty's memory of this period is likely also clouded by her own difficult relationship with her father. They were not close, and to a degree Lefty even feared him. She believes her father caused hardships for her mother, and she is not at all convinced that her mother was happy with the respect that was born out of the fear that her father commanded in their community.

Whether or not Virtudes was happy with such a grudging respect is unclear, but she nonetheless used it to carve out at least some semblance of a middle-class life. As Lefty remembers, "[At least during that time] we were what my other wanted us to be: respectable." They could not afford expensive clothes, but Lefty remembers that her mother always looked nice. "Rich people gave clothes to my mother, and no matter what, my mother always looked respectable. That was so important to her. Then she made it important for me, only I didn't care like she did." It seemed the family was always one step behind when trying to establish itself as solidly middle class. Whether it was Virtudes's clothes or the neighborhood in which they lived, they were just out of reach of the comfort Virtudes so desperately wanted.

The family lived in El Cerro, a one-time summer retreat for Havana's Creole aristocracy. In the 1920s the elite of Cuba built mansions along the wide streets of the barrio, each more elaborate than the next. Because of the economic depression and the political revolutions of the 1930s, however, the area began to fall into decline. The rich moved out, and poorer families began to move into the area. The Álvarez family was one of the new arrivals. Lefty said, "[For my family] this was a fancy neighborhood, and my mother was proud to be here. I don't think she knew, or maybe didn't care, that it was not the area for rich people any more. She could pretend. She pretended a lot." Virtudes not only pretended, but also simply ignored the family's financial situation and allowed Lefty to do the same until Batista lost power in 1944. After Batista's ouster nearly anyone with ties to him and his government became unemployed and unemployable. Prudencio "went to the place he worked, and they stripped him of his uniform, everything, and that was it. He was without a job," Lefty recalls. Perhaps even more disturbing for Virtudes, Batista supporters were also shunned by society. For Virtudes respect from the community was important; when that faded because of Prudencio's connection to Batista, it was that loss that hit her the hardest—at least until the family felt the full effects of Prudencio's unemployment.

Virtudes once again found herself on a path she did not want and had not expected when she and Prudencio had married. Lefty remembers that her parents seemed to be on different sides after that time. It was not a political separation but a personal one. They were not like a family, Lefty remembers: "My mother was very mad, and she blamed [Prudencio], not Batista, for losing his job. She would yell at him, and he would just leave." This sentiment was echoed by Antonio as well, although he did not remember that time with as much sadness as Lefty does. "Tony told me that our parents did not talk much and that our father would stay home doing nothing during the day, then get all dressed up and leave at night. He did not see anything wrong with that," Lefty remembers.

With no income for the family, Virtudes had to go to work. Lefty sees this as her father and brother taking advantage of Virtudes. She remembers bitterly that not only Prudencio, but also Tony "didn't care when our mother had to get a job in a match factory just a few blocks from home. It was very hard work, and then when she came home with her fingers all burned, she had to wait on my father and brother all the time. It was like she was their slave, always having to fix meals and clean up after them." Lefty's alliance with her mother raises questions about her one-sided view of this dynamic. But clearly Virtudes's hopes of a better life were slipping away, and she did not tolerate an unemployed husband for long. Eventually she demanded that Prudencio get a job as well, any job. As Lefty remembers, she demanded, "Clean the streets for all I care. Just get a job! I'm hungry." Lefty vividly remembers her parents fighting about this issue. Her father said, "You want people to see me clean the streets?" Virtudes responded, "I don't care; just get a job."

Swallowing his pride, Prudencio got a job at a bank for what he hoped to be a temporary stint, although he would not return to Batista's police force. Lefty refers to him as a janitor but also talks about other odd jobs Prudencio did for the bank. It was low-status work, but he kept the job until his retirement. The fact that he remained at the bank caused an even greater divide between Prudencio and Virtudes. "The lack of love between them seemed more obvious to me," Lefty says. Given Virtudes's quest for respectability and a solidly middle-class existence for her family, it is not surprising that Prudencio's inability to provide them would cause a greater rift between them.

In these ways the political and economic turmoil in Cuba cast the family into the working class, the very status Virtudes had sought to avoid. The loss of middle-class respectability dominated the rest of Virtudes's life and shaped her relationship with her daughter. Her determination that Lefty would live a better life replaced Virtudes's goals for herself and consequently took over Lefty's life. Virtudes wanted Lefty to have the life that she had failed to find.

To this end Virtudes seems to have protected Lefty from the family's more serious personal and financial struggles. Despite their descent into the working class and Virtudes's anger over that fact, she worked to create a different reality for her daughter. Virtudes's daily life was anything but middle class; she had to work outside the home and very obviously could not afford the fine clothes middle-class women wore. Her husband, now a bank janitor, no longer represented the middle-class status she thought he would provide for her. Yet she insisted that they, Virtudes and Lefty, were better than working class. Time after time Virtudes urged Lefty to have a middle-class consciousness. "My mother always told me that no matter what, I would be somebody. [She said,] 'You should never hang around riffraff. We are better than that.'" Almost willing it to be so, Virtudes created for Lefty the illusion of the middle-class life she herself desired. The reality of their lives, however, was quite different.

Prudencio's life, from orphan to the son of a priest and from a member of Batista's police force to bank janitor, was filled with nearly as many successes as failures, but in the eyes of Virtudes, he had simply failed. For a time Prudencio was able to provide Virtudes with the middle-class prestige she so desired, but when economic and political turmoil gripped Cuba, that ended and she was back where she had begun, seeking respectability. Her frustration with his failures led to arguments and eventually to estrangement, and even though they stayed married and lived in the same house, Virtudes gave up on her husband. Pinning her own hopes and dreams on her daughter, Virtudes set out to make Lefty "a grand Cuban success."

CHAPTER TWO

Refashioning Lefty

I was always confused about what to do. Play ball or wear pretty dresses. My mother chose for me, and I am glad she chose sports.

LEFTY ALVAREZ

For Lefty's mother life in Cuba had been full of struggles. She had to fight for enough money and food, let alone to achieve even a fraction of the middle-class respectability she desperately wanted. Worried that her daughter might suffer similar problems, Virtudes set out to refashion a life for Lefty that would bring her opportunity and respect. Because the family struggled financially, Virtudes knew that Lefty's status could never be elevated because of wealth. Cuban women faced dismal employment and educational prospects, and no one knew this more keenly than Virtudes. For Lefty to overcome the hardships of a working-class life in Cuba, Virtudes would need to be creative, and she was. Virtudes took Lefty down many different paths—radio shows, beauty pageants, and several kinds of sports—in her effort to help her overcome the depressing prospects most Cuban women faced. Not only did Virtudes help Lefty overcome the family's bleak financial situation, but she also helped her to do something few Cuban women could do: beat a social system stacked firmly against women.

As noted in the previous chapter, throughout the nineteenth and early twentieth centuries opportunities for economic, educational, and social advancement were limited for Cuba's women. Eventually Cuban women realized that if they were going to gain any level of equality, they must seize on popular revolutionary sentiment, which openly challenged the inequities of class and race. For women to attain even a modicum of the social, economic, and political equality revolutionaries sought, they had to organize. As was true around the world, feminist movements in Cuba were effective only after activists had created organizations focused on issues of larger national concerns. Cuban feminists launched their fight for equality alongside those who fought for worker's rights, better living conditions, increased educational opportunities, and higher wages. Within that context of widespread revolution women highlighted the inequities they faced and forged political alliances.[1] Within such a context women's organizations and the issues on which they focused became increasingly visible.

Early Cuban feminists focused their efforts on political change, political access to women, and women's right to vote. Among the first feminist organizations was the Comité de Sufragio Femenino. It was established in 1912 and was organized to push for increased political participation among women. Patterned in part on the National Women's Suffrage Association of the United States, this organization focused almost exclusively on women's suffrage and women's political involvement. Eventually the tactics and the focus among feminists broadened; one result was the establishment of the Club Femenino de Cuba, created in 1917. Unlike the Comité de Sufragio Femenino, the Club formed around a variety of social issues such as prostitution, the establishment of separate women's prisons, and women's voting rights. Seeking coordinated political action that would benefit women, the Club organized the first National Women's Congress in Havana in April 1923. Organizers combined "nationalism, commitment to motherhood and the family, and women's rights as the motivating factors of the Cuban woman's rights movement."[2] They passed resolutions demanding the right to vote, equal rights for women under the law, and an expansion of educational opportunities for women.[3]

Like feminist organizations worldwide, groups in Cuba were often split along race or class lines. In 1921 elite women from Cuban society created the Asociación Femenina de Camagüey. This group published Cuba's first feminist journal, the *Asociación de Damas Isabelinas*. The journal was conceived as a social, literary, and feminist magazine. The Asociación Femenina de Camagüey was not an overly political group but worked to create opportunities for women through literature and education, and it primarily appealed to the middle- and upper-class women of Cuba.

While education was often pushed as a tool for change, tactics varied and results were mixed. Many women supported traditional political values and often involved themselves in resource allocations and projects set aside for them within the departments of education, health, and welfare. Feminists who believed education was crucial to improving women's status were often forced to settle for just a mention of education in a very crowded political agenda.[4] Despite a lack of widespread political support from male leaders for increasing educational options for girls and women, advances continued at a steady, if not rapid, pace throughout the early twentieth century. Due in large part to the efforts of women's organizations, illiteracy rates for girls and women declined from 58 percent in 1899 to 39 percent in 1919. In cities such as Havana and Santiago female literacy rates grew at a faster rate than in the rural areas of the country. Within a few years of reformers' push to educate girls, literacy rates rose to 84 percent in Havana and 83 percent in Santiago.[5] Much of this increase was due to the growing Cuban women's movement.

These educational changes offered young girls of Lefty's generation a few more opportunities than their mothers had had. Still most families at that time did not have the same educational goals for daughters as they had for sons. Like most Cuban girls in the 1930s and 1940s, Lefty was expected to attend school only to learn the basics: reading, writing, and math. Virtudes was dedicated to helping Lefty reach a level of respectability that Virtudes believed was synonymous with that of the middle class. But because she herself had grown up poor and in a very traditional household, Virtudes had had few educational opportunities and therefore did not see education as a necessary road to success for her daughter.

Virtudes's attitude about Lefty's schooling may also have been shaped by her daughter's experience as a student. Lefty had a miserable time in elementary school, and schoolwork petrified her. Lefty recalls how hard it was to read, study, and sit still in class: "I had an inferiority complex. . . . I was scared to death when I had an examination; I got so nervous, so sick, that I could not do the work. Oh, the time limits! You had to answer in an hour." Given her reaction, it is not surprising that Lefty was not a strong student. But when she came home with stories of fear and incompetence, her parents just encouraged her to try harder. Perhaps because girls were simply not taken seriously as students, neither her parents nor Lefty's teachers dug for answers to Lefty's issues in school.

Lefty remembers that "In school I panicked and was so nervous. I couldn't wait until it was break time." Yet freedom from classes did not solve all her problems. It wasn't just the work that was hard for Lefty. The social aspects were also alienating. Finding friends was difficult. She failed to fit in with the other girls in part because she failed to do what was expected of young women her age. "All that playing of girl's games, cooking, flirting with boys, or primping—I just couldn't do it. I hated it, but it meant I didn't have friends." Her insecurity about her ability to learn also got in the way. "I was always slow—you know, not very smart in school—which made me shy," she explains. "Because I wasn't smart, no one wanted to be my friend, so I was also lonely, except when I was out playing ball." Baseball had already become important to Lefty. It would just take a while to see how crucial the game would be.

Lefty did everything in her power to get out of school. Eventually her problems became too great to ignore. Lefty had developed asthma. Her fear and anxiety over school worsened, and because of the asthma, Lefty often struggled to breathe. This was especially a problem at school. When Lefty was about ten years old, her doctors told Virtudes to keep her home from school for the entire year. When Lefty found out about this, she immediately felt better. "That year was the best time, my happiest time. I didn't get asthma at home, and I could go out and play ball. My mother tutored me some, and I learned more that way than I ever did in school."

Virtudes's willingness to keep Lefty out of school came from a place of love and support, but it also showed Virtudes's inability to understand the importance of education. Lefty remembers that her mother was not really concerned about her not going to school. "It's okay," Lefty remembers her mother telling her. "I could be something without it." Even though she was happy to be excused from school for a period, Lefty did not understand why she was so afraid of school or why she had such a hard time learning. In hindsight Lefty thinks she likely had a learning disability. Whatever the reason, Lefty did not do well in school, and Virtudes saw no reason to push her. Years later, when she struggled to find employment, Lefty would feel some betrayal because her mother had failed to understand or address her daughter's academic troubles.

While she did not seek to understand the reasons, Virtudes realized that education was not Lefty's strong suit and that she would never be able to use it as a path out of Cuba. So Virtudes sought other ways for Lefty to overcome poverty that did not require an education. Lefty was a very attractive young girl, and initially Virtudes thought that Lefty's ticket out of the working class was her beauty. As in other Latin American countries in the twentieth century, beauty pageants were popular in Cuba, and they were often seen as a way out of poverty by families with daughters. In pre-revolutionary Cuba beauty pageants were widely organized, and some attractive women did change their lives for the better as a result of them. Because the participants could earn money and a level of local fame, the pageants gave some working-class families a boost to the middle class. Aware of these facts and without Lefty's knowledge, Virtudes entered her daughter in a local beauty contest. "She just told me I was going to do it, that it was one way out of this life," Lefty recalls." Lefty always trusted her mother and did not doubt her ever: "If my mother told me to do something, I did it. I did not question [her] because I trusted her. I trusted she wanted the best for me always."

Lefty had very little time to prepare, physically or emotionally, for the pageant, and the experience was most definitely not a positive one for her. Years later her clearest memories are of the ways in which her mother pushed and angled for every possible advantage. In one incident Lefty recalls that as she was about to walk on stage, Virtudes pulled her aside to "stuff my bra with Kleenex. Guess she thought that would draw attention." It likely did. Lefty was only thirteen or fourteen at the time (she is unsure of her exact age), but she remembers that she was "not very top-heavy." Even though she finished second in that contest, Lefty was unhappy with the experience: "I was miserable playing like I was just a lady, sitting around looking pretty. I wanted to please my mother, so I did what she asked, but it was not good for me to pretend." As Lefty's unhappiness grew, her ability to hide her sadness, uneasiness, and anxiety from Virtudes diminished.

Virtudes realized the toll the pageants were taking on Lefty, so she abandoned them as a path out of poverty. She never stopped trying to get Lefty out of El Cerro, however.

Some of Virtudes's actions during this period seem to contradict her focus on Lefty's respectability and even to threaten her daughter's well-being. But for Virtudes respectability was primarily about appearance. After realizing that Lefty's personality was not suited to the world of beauty pageants, Virtudes turned to radio and television work as another possibility for Lefty's future. Lefty remarks: "I guess she thought I was pretty, and maybe a future husband or employer, someone rich or important, would see me announcing or doing commercials. I did not show interest in these things. I was shy and did not want to be in the center . . . unless I was playing games on the street." Despite Lefty's age (again she is unsure of her exact age but thinks it was between thirteen and fifteen), a lack of interest in broadcasting of any kind, and the fact that she simply did not have the personality for such a job, Virtudes set up an interview for Lefty at a local radio station. She was to meet a man who they both thought was going to help Lefty get into this new career. Lefty describes the situation: "He worked at the radio station. I don't remember his name. All I remember is that he was big and fat. He sat me down in front of the microphone to train me in how to talk on the radio, and as he motioned with his hand up and down to indicate how loud my voice should be, he touched my breasts. I still feel it; it was my left breast, his right hand. I went home crying and told my mother I did not want to do that anymore." All these years later Lefty remembers the experience with pain and embarrassment. Still careful to never speak badly of her mother, Lefty did not openly accuse her mother of exploitation. In retelling this story, however, Lefty asked over and over, "Why did she do that? She had to know." Virtudes had to know that she was not sending Lefty to a job interview. Lefty was not going to be a radio announcer at age thirteen. She was too young and had no experience.

Despite that knowledge, it was Lefty's failure to secure the job that most upset Virtudes, not the sexual assault she suffered. "I tried to tell [my mother] more about that meeting, but she just kept telling me I had messed up and that he was only going to help us. Us? Help us? He did not touch my mother. How would he help us?" There is no doubt Virtudes loved Lefty and tried desperately to help lift her from a life of poverty, but even after Lefty told her mother about the assault and Virtudes realized Lefty's fear and confusion, she set up another situation that clearly put Lefty in danger.

This incident took place in a dentist's office. Thinking that Virtudes was still focused on her looks and the use of her beauty to help her find a way out of poverty, Lefty went willingly to a dentist appointment her mother had arranged. The dentist was a man Virtudes knew. He promised to help the family, although it is not clear exactly what that help would be. Lefty says, "I thought then that it was because she wanted me to be beautiful and thought my teeth were important. I don't know, but I went like she told me to." It turned out to be more complicated. Lefty continues:

> I do not know why I had to go there. I never had a problem with my teeth, but she just kept saying he would help us. She sent me there with no money. I thought it was going to be free. She didn't go with me, just sent me there with no money. That was strange. She did not like me to go places without her. Once I got in the chair, he started touching me. I didn't like it but was afraid and did not scream or anything. I did not tell him to stop. My mother, whom I always listened to, had told me to go. So I did and was just silent. Before I left, he gave me seventeen dollars. I went home upset but did not tell anybody until [I am now telling] you. I just gave my mother the seventeen dollars.

As in retelling the story about the radio interview, Lefty kept asking why. Why would her mother do these things to her? Insisting that she had to have known what the men were going to do, Lefty remains hurt and confused. Thankful that her mother was determined that Lefty should have a different life than the one she had lived but still smarting from what she sees as a betrayal by Virtudes, Lefty is both angry with and perplexed by her mother's tactics. It was after Lefty's visit to the dentist that her father and brother, who had been kept out of the plans for Lefty's life, voiced open disapproval. "I just don't understand why she did it. Even my brother and father were confused by her actions," Lefty observes. They told Virtudes that it was wrong to send such a young girl to such places alone. Nothing, not Lefty's tear or the rebuke of her husband or son, weakened Virtudes's determination, however.

While there can be no doubt that Virtudes loved her daughter and set out to protect her, Lefty was also protective of and devoted to her mother. They relied on each other while Lefty was still in Cuba. When Lefty was a young girl, her mother depended upon her when her own frailties surfaced. Lefty remembers her mother's terrible headaches and how they so debilitated her:

> When she had one of those headaches, she always wanted me to lie with her in the bed. I could not lie on my back or have my back to her. We always had to lie facing each other. I did not like it, and my father even told her not to do it anymore. But we did anyway. My mother said yes, and my father said no. I was so afraid and did not know what to do. I was a kid. I would just lie there listening for my father to come home and would jump up.

Lefty was uncomfortable with her mother's insistence that she lie next to her and later described feeling exploited. She questioned her mother's actions, stating, "I was only a child, and she should not have done that to me. How could I say no to my mother?" Making this experience even more difficult and confusing, Lefty's brother accused them of "being lesbians together." Lefty was confused and embarrassed by Tony's accusation: "I did not know what he meant then. I did not understand, but my mother did, and she was very mad. I think that is when she stopped liking my brother." Eventually Lefty did understand what her brother was implying, and she was horrified. Lefty's anger was transferred from her mother for insisting she lie with her to Tony for accusing them of incest.

As upset as Lefty was with her brother, it was another incident that both solidified her mistrust of Tony and created an uneasy relationship with sexuality. She explains: "There is a lot I am not sure is okay to say, but one time, I was very young, and he was taking a shower. He asked me to get in with him. Why he did it I do not know. I was young and I knew it was wrong, so I did not go." She did tell her parents, however. After this incident Lefty was not allowed to sleep in the same room as her brother. She slept in the room with her mother, and Prudencio slept with Tony. Later Lefty remembers with regret that "after I told about this, my brother could never even put an arm on my shoulder as normal people do, and I felt guilty. So did he, I think, but even now I feel guilty. Why?!" From that time forward Lefty's mother told her that Tony was "no good" and that she should never trust him. She never did. Even though Virtudes's actions were equally exploitative, she managed to convince Lefty to blame Tony and not her. Instead Virtudes convinced Lefty that she alone knew what was best for her and that in time she would help Lefty out of poverty and out of Cuba.

Virtudes was steadfast, and when neither the beauty pageant route nor the radio route panned out as potential careers for Lefty, her mother turned to Lefty's athleticism. After years of trying to find just the right path—the one that fit both her own middle-class sensibilities and Lefty's interests and talents—Virtudes finally realized that Lefty's ticket to respectability and to the United States was sport. Virtudes was a lifelong baseball fan who had learned to play on the streets of her neighborhood in El Cerro. Despite Virtudes's love of the game and Lefty's interest in and talent for the game, initially Virtudes did not see baseball as an acceptable path for her daughter. Baseball was not tied to the middle class or to the ideas of beauty and respectability Virtudes held dear. She turned instead to sports that were linked with the middle class and the elite.

In the pre-Castro revolution period sports, like most things in Cuba, were divided by class. Organized sports were not provided for the lower classes, who were generally left to entertain themselves in their leisure time with sports such as boxing, gambling (in the form of horse and dog racing), cockfighting, jai alai pelota (a game played in a three-walled court with a ball and hand-held device called a cesta), dice games, and baseball.[6] Cockfighting, which was perhaps the most popular sport for the working class, had been a part of Cuban culture from the early nineteenth century, and despite being outlawed after the War for Cuban Independence, it continued to be very popular. By the mid-1940s there was a large web of gambling events centered on cockfighting, and the crowds had become large.[7] Small farmers bred cockerels for fighting, and whether by selling them or entering them in contests, they made a great deal of money. What all of these games and sports had in common was that they required little in the way of equipment or formal training, making them accessible to the lower classes in Cuba.

For the wealthy classes most sports were controlled by private interests, and an abundance of recreational opportunities existed. Games and sports such as billiards, fishing, and swimming (as well as loosely organized activities such as concerts, dances, and horseback riding) were in abundance. For those who wanted to compete in organized sports, sailing and tennis clubs (among others) were established, while wealthy youth had access to sports at school and at the University of Havana.[8] Since the privileged classes were the only ones with leisure time and access to sports clubs, it was only they who reached a level of expertise necessary to play on Cuba's organized amateur sports teams.

The class divide in sports was not limited to urban areas such as Havana. In the rural areas of Cuba similar sports clubs were established by U.S.-owned companies, further accenting the class and racial discrimination in Cuban sports. For example, on the United Fruit sugar plantation there was one sports club for American citizens and one for Cuban workers. A sugar mill worker, Angel Leiba Cabrera, remembers, "When the Americans were here, they had these three recreational centers, one just for Americans; . . . I couldn't put my face in there. . . . The Pan-American Club—the one for Americans—had a swimming pool, but of course it was only for them."[9] Whether they were privately sponsored or American-business sponsored, sports clubs in both urban and rural areas went a long way in maintaining the racial and class hierarchy of Cuba.

In addition to the race and class divide, sports were also segregated by gender. The activities of Cuban women were very limited, so many of the sports clubs were for men only. Exercise for women tended to be less organized and included strolls in the park, horseback riding, and the occasional dance at a social club. During the late nineteenth and early twentieth centuries immigrants to Cuba, especially the Criollos (ethnic Spaniards born outside Spain) brought with them new ideas about women's participation in sport. They were also responsible for creating more sports clubs. That increase opened the way for women to participate in acceptable sports such as cycling, tennis, fencing, and volleyball.

Virtudes watched closely as more sporting opportunities opened for girls. She knew her daughter shined in nearly every sport she attempted and that Lefty herself was happier when competing. Playing childhood games on the streets of El Cerro is among Lefty's favorite memories. From the age of six or seven Lefty was focused on outdoor games: "I was the only girl that played games in my neighborhood, she says. Despite being the only girl, Lefty was a leader and often the winner of those kids' games. She loved "to be out on the street playing pelota, playing marbles, climbing trees, or stealing mangos and lemons off trees." It didn't matter what the game or sport was, she excelled. She reminisces that playing games on the streets of her neighborhood earned her the title of "*la pilla del Cerro* [the rascal of El Cerro]. . . . The neighbors gave me the title of *la pilla del Cerro* because I was always out on the street playing baseball and showing off." Lefty's time playing such games was acceptable to Virtudes until sport became the focus of her plan for Lefty. Then she became more conscious of the games Lefty played. Those games were not the sports of the middle class, so Virtudes set out to transform Lefty's athletic life. The focus had to shift to the sports played by "the right people."

Always aware of what the wealthy were doing and how they were represented even in sports, Virtudes eventually forbade Lefty from playing those street games and encouraged her to fence and play volleyball or soccer, sports that were most often played by the wealthy classes. Lefty enjoyed and excelled at both volleyball and fencing but did not always understand the ways in which those sports represented class. "I loved to play volleyball," she says. "That was my best sport really—oh, and fencing. I liked that too, but the people [in both volleyball and fencing], they did not like me." Lefty's volleyball teammates' dislike of her may well have been based on class. Despite her mother's belief that playing the right sports would make Lefty middle class, Lefty experienced class discrimination when playing the more exclusive sports.

Fencing was a very exclusive sport and began as an organized activity in 1891 with the establishment of Havana's fencing club, Club Gimnastico. By the time Lefty was learning to fence, the sport was firmly entrenched as an acceptable leisure-time activity for the upper classes. She began this sport before Prudencio was fired from the Batista police force but continued to fence even after he became a janitor. While they were not considered wealthy when he worked for Batista, the family enjoyed a level of respect in the community (as noted above). Likely Virtudes parlayed that into opportunities for Lefty: "I remember my mother going one day to talk to a man about me learning to do fencing." Unlike the games she played on the streets, "it was well organized, and directing the fencing were people from the government."[10] Because the government was involved, there were more possibilities for expansion in the sport. Lefty remembers her mother's insistence that "fencing was also more appropriate for ladies and that is what I should always be, even when playing sports. A lady."

Despite Lefty's reservations, Virtudes's strong will won, and Lefty learned to fence. But she was unsure about fencing: "I did not know about it as a sport, but my mother said I should be good at it. She took me to what I call a gym now, and [the teacher] taught me to fence, but the other people did not talk to me. It was not like the games I liked to play where I had friends and people saw I was good." While fencing, Lefty was not the *pilla*, the rascal, she was when she ran the streets of her neighborhood. She was not comfortable, and even though she turned out to be good at fencing, her mother could tell this was not Lefty's sport: "My mother told me one day that we were not going to keep doing this. I also played volleyball and soccer at the same time, and she wanted me to focus on those sports." Even though Virtudes had shifted her attention from Lefty's physical appearance to her athletic ability, she kept a close watch on the sports Lefty played. She understood that even sports were a class identifier in 1940s Cuba; if she was going to create a middle-class life for Lefty, even the sports she played would have to measure up. Soccer and volleyball, like fencing, were acceptable.

As noted, both volleyball and soccer in Cuba were generally run by private clubs and usually by individuals who were either European or European-educated Cubans. One example was the soccer-focused Hatuey Sport Club established in the center of Havana. The club led the way in creating other soccer teams and organizations in Cuba; eventually Cuba's soccer association joined the international soccer federation. (FIFA). Cuba participated in the 1938 World Cup, and many of Europe's most successful soccer clubs came to Cuba for matches.[11] Soccer was never as popular in Cuba as it was in other Latin American countries, but a lighted soccer stadium was built just outside Havana in 1928. Such a stadium illustrates the extent to which the wealthy supported the sport. The stadium was paid for by the president of Club Deportivo Hispano-Americano, a Spaniard who owned a confectionary factory.[12] Virtudes was aware of the country's European connection to soccer and the fact that it was a game for the wealthy. She encouraged Lefty to play. As Lefty herself remembers, "I was good at it, like most sports, but it just seemed like she wanted me to play to get to know the people. I was not interested in that part; it was just the game for me." Neither Lefty's soccer career nor her fencing, volleyball, or basketball careers provided the path out of poverty that Virtudes had hoped they would. Virtudes did not take into account one very important fact: while Lefty was good at those sports, it was baseball that she loved and that provided her with the "best time of my life, the days playing baseball on the streets of El Cerro." Because she loved baseball, loved to play it, watch it, and learn about it, Lefty was far more likely to be good at it and to maintain the focus needed to be successful at it.

Eventually Virtudes, a lifelong baseball fan herself, realized that baseball was not only Lefty's ticket out of poverty, but also her ticket to happiness. Following a long Cuban and family tradition, Lefty not only loved the game of baseball, but she also relied on it for solace and strength. During her long journey from the streets of Havana to the pitcher's mound at Wrigley Field in Chicago, Lefty relied on what she called good "sporting stock." Good, Cuban, baseball "sporting stock." Lefty concludes: "I know my country's baseball history, and now I know I am part of that too. I did not know it then, but now I see it was that good stock that helped me. It was baseball all along."

CHAPTER THREE

The Passion of the Island

In my country, we all love baseball. Especially my mother. She lit candles and prayed for her team when they played. Oh my, she loved them.

LEFTY ALVAREZ

On a sunny Havana street youngsters gather to play a version of baseball called *cuatro esquinas* (four corners). The same kids show up nearly every day with their "ball"—a rock wrapped in white medical tape—and a tree branch for a bat. In this game there are no gloves and no base running. Either players hit the ball over the fielder's head or they are out. Even though it is very different from the game played by their national heroes, street ball is where would-be professionals hone their skills in the hope that they will eventually be chosen for one of Cuba's prestigious baseball academies. Most know there is little chance they will make it that far, but that does not keep them from dreaming of a life in professional baseball. Imagine those young ballplayers, wide-eyed, sweating, and proud as they step up to the plate, pretending they are playing in front of thousands at Havana stadium. It is the bottom of the ninth inning, and they, with one swing, can win the game. The pitch is right down the middle. Crack! Imagine the satisfaction as the ball sails over the make-believe left-field wall. Now imagine that those ballplayers are girls.

Those imagined girls playing baseball in the imagined Gran Stadium of Havana represent a long Cuban tradition: a love for the game of baseball. Arguably baseball is the most popular sport on the island and has been for over a century.[1] The game was introduced to Cuba in the 1860s by Cuban brothers Nemesio and Ernesto Guillot. They attended Spring Hill College in Mobile, Alabama, and there they were introduced to baseball. When they returned to Cuba in 1864, they brought with them a bat and a ball. At the time, other sports were popular in Cuba, but most, such as bullfighting, were either spectator sports for the wealthy or games like tennis, fencing, or volleyball, which were played in clubs catering to the wealthy classes. The game of baseball, however, was soon embraced by all classes of Cubans. All that was needed to play the game was a bat of some sort, a ball, and some imagination. The widespread acceptance of the sport quickly made baseball the most popular game on the island. Within a few years a group of sportsmen, including the Guillot brothers, formed the first organized baseball team in Cuba, the Club Habana de Béisbol (the Havana Base Ball Club).[2] The club became popular, and its members began traveling to other parts of Cuba to play baseball. In 1869 they traveled to Matanzas, where they played the crew of an American schooner anchored at the Matanzas harbor.[3] Despite their relative newness to the game and the fact that baseball had come to them from the United States, they defeated the American sailors. The win was a boost to the club's reputation and to Cuba's interest in baseball.

Baseball became so popular that it created a problem. Cubans were expected to embrace Spanish culture, all aspects of it, including sports. Bullfighting was especially important to the colonial government as a sort of homage to the Spanish. When the attendance at bullfights began to wane, Cuba's rulers blamed the growing popularity of baseball, a decidedly non-Spanish game. In 1869, with rebellion brewing on the island, the Spanish officially banned baseball. But by then it was too late, and the ban would not be strongly enforced or outlast the conflict. The game was already tied to Cuban identity, and Spanish efforts to stop its growth made it a symbol of freedom and egalitarianism to the Cuban people. In fact, through all of the years of revolution that followed, baseball was one constant that held Cubans, if not their country, together.

Over the next two decades the game flourished. On the streets, in abandoned fields, and eventually within organized clubs around the country, Cubans continued to play baseball. The creation of Cuba's first organized baseball competition further solidified it as Cuba's game. In what is believed to be the first competition between two organized clubs, Club Matanzas and Club Habana played in Pueblo Nuevo, Matanzas, at the Palmar del

Junco, on December 27, 1874. Those teams became the foundation of the professional Cuban League, and that game is thought to be the league's first.[4] Originally the league consisted of three teams: Almendares, Havana, and Matanzas. The league grew, and eventually the national professional baseball competition emerged. Further professionalizing the game, championships were played between teams from various Cuban leagues, giving the winner of the championship national credibility.

Just as Cuba's enthusiasm for baseball grew, so did Spain's distrust of it. Not only did baseball become Cuba's national pastime, but also, as noted, it became a tool for and a symbol of Cuban independence. Confirming Spain's fears, in 1895 officials discovered that profits from baseball were being diverted to the independence movement supported by José Martí, so once again baseball was banned in Cuba.[5] As had happened in 1869, the second Spanish ban on baseball only added to the game's popularity and to Cubans' determination to play, watch, and financially support it. They did all three. By the turn of the twentieth century and the beginnings of U.S. cultural influence, baseball was well established as the preferred sport of the Cuban people. Cubans were passionate about the game, to the point that fans of rival teams often had to be kept separated in stadiums.[6] It mattered to them whose teams won games because baseball mattered. In the process of rejecting Spanish rule, Cubans had embraced "America's game" and turned baseball into a symbol of Cuban pride.

In 1898, after the War for Cuban Independence, the United States replaced Spain as the occupier of Cuba. A complicated political and economic relationship developed between Cuba and the United States in the first thirty years of the twentieth century, and the U.S. presence in Cuba immediately after the island's declaration of independence caused great concerns. There was no denying the importance of the United States to the economic well-being of Cuba, but many Cubans were leery. Some warned against the possibility of the United States' becoming another imperial power controlling their country's political and financial future. Others—those who owned sugar mills and other Cuban industries important to U.S. economic interests—continued to support the physical and economic presence of the United States on the island. All agreed, however, that baseball, the sport brought from up north, transformed in Cuba, and used to symbolize independence from Spain had ironically benefited the most from the U.S. occupation.

It is no coincidence that the years between 1898 and 1930, when the United States had a strong presence on the island, are often referred to as "the Golden Age" of baseball in Cuba.[7] In that period the game grew on many levels. First, the popularity of amateur baseball continued to spread throughout the country. Baseball continued to be played by nearly every class, in most neighborhoods and provinces, and by all ages. Amateur baseball continued to grow and reached its peak in the decade of the 1940s. Sugar mills supported their own baseball teams, and these had the greatest national growth in this period because they were tied to Cuba's largest industry, so the teams played in every province. Sugar mill teams accounted for many of the teams in Cuba's amateur leagues. Their players were role models to many young Cubans who grew up playing the game, or some version of it, on the streets.[8]

Semiprofessional baseball, which included teams sponsored by industries of all types and were open to everyone (including former professional players), grew during this period as well. Many players and coaches nearing the end of their careers found a home in these semiprofessional teams. The growth of professional baseball in Cuba during the "Golden Age" was itself unprecedented. In this period Cubans competed regularly against the best players from the U.S. Major Leagues and Negro Leagues. This competition made the Cuban players better, and when they won such games, fans responded with enthusiasm and crowds swelled.

While the first thirty years of the twentieth century are known as the "Golden Age" of baseball, some significant changes occurred during the 1940s and 1950s as well. After suffering financial loses and a decline in popularity during the Depression, the Cuban League was revived in the early 1940s. Teams benefited from increased financial investments, the Gran Stadium was completed in 1946, and the Cuban League began admitting black players. Within a short time players from the North American Negro Leagues moved to Cuba and began playing on Cuba's integrated teams.[9] This expansion provided new opportunities for players, fans, and investors. Each of these moves helped to increase the fan base and the financial well-being and popularity of the game. Cubans—rich, poor, men, women, and children—loved the game of baseball. As a result of new investments their opportunities to play and watch the game also grew. Whether their allegiance was to the local amateur leagues, the industrial teams represented by the growing sugar mill leagues, or the now more established professional league, Cubans were dedicated to their game. This is the baseball world in which Lefty grew up.

Cuban weather in February is nearly perfect for baseball. The air is cool, and the sun is bright but not yet oppressive. Even though Cuban baseball fans of the 1940s and 1950s would line up to see their favorite teams in the stifling heat and humidity of summer, on February winter days the stadiums overflowed with spectators.[10] Even for a late afternoon game fans nearly filled the stands by mid-morning, and a carnival-like atmosphere existed, with hawkers selling their wares and gamblers advertising their odds for the day's game. Spectators spilled out onto the field, with only rope separating them from the players. Many fans stood on the streets outside the stadium so that they could hear the public address announcer call the game, and even more listened to the games on radios from their homes. On a baseball afternoon in Cuba the game punctuated the day. It drew friends, neighbors, and families together and gave even those with the most difficult lives a brief reprieve from hardship.

Lefty and her family were among those who both loved and relied on baseball. Lefty remembers "my mother in the kitchen, all by herself, with candles lit, praying while she listened to the baseball game on the radio. We lived close to the stadium [Gran Stadium], and she could open the windows and hear the cheers of the fans there. She loved it so." In the shadow of that stadium, where the energy, excitement, and sounds of baseball permeated the neighborhood, Lefty Alvarez learned to appreciate the game. "We loved it," Lefty said. "We all loved the game, not just my mother. I loved to play and watch or listen, and I especially loved the sound of it."

Lefty not only watched baseball, but she also played it. But the street version that Lefty and the neighborhood kids played was very different from what we recognize as baseball today. Lefty fondly recalls how they made their own balls: "We collected old cigarette boxes from the garbage, tore them into strips, and wrapped them into a ball shape." They used their hands for bats; it was not until she began playing for the Cuban women's team that Lefty got her first baseball glove. Yet those games on the streets of Havana were crucial in forming Lefty's identity and her sense of self. Playing baseball helped to build the strength it took Lefty to survive a very difficult and, at times, lonely life. Sports were a refuge for Lefty, a place where she felt comfortable, good, and free, feelings that nothing else provided her. But it was baseball, the game she loved and played on the streets of El Cerro, that provided Lefty with a lifeline and her mother with another plan.

When Virtudes finally realized that none of the more acceptable, middle-class-approved sports or a career in radio or beauty pageants were going to get Lefty out of poverty, she turned to baseball. A huge fan of the game herself, Virtudes allowed Lefty to play baseball on their neighborhood streets but never paid much attention to how well Lefty played in those children's games. It wasn't until 1947, when Virtudes learned that a new women's baseball league was being developed in Cuba, that she turned her attention to Lefty's baseball ability.

In late 1946, according to Lefty, "a group of sports loving Cubans" led by Rafael de León had begun recruiting for a Cuban women's baseball team that would be called the Estrellas Cubanas (Cuban Stars).[11] De León was a wealthy beer and wine merchant in Havana with business connections to the AAGPBL's Philip K. Wrigley and Max Carey. He worked with the North Americans to develop his team as a Latin American branch of the women's league. "Working in close cooperation with Max Carey and other AA League Officials, the Latin American loop was patterned after Carey's organization. The All-American game, known as Girls' Baseball, was adopted along with all of the AA rules and regulations."[12] De León built a baseball field, trained the players, and on weekends housed them at his own ranch so that they would not have to go home.

Lefty was unsure how her mother even found out about the new team. Before she understood what was happening, she was on her way to tryouts for the Cuban team. As she remembers it, "One day I was down in the streets playing ball with my brother and my mother came, and she took me to an organized baseball team in Havana." Lefty attended those tryouts without a glove and with only the experience of playing baseball on the streets of El Cerro. Her mother said, "Play." So she played, and the experience changed her life. Despite her youth and inexperience, at the age of thirteen Lefty made the team. She remembers the experience and de León fondly. He believed in her talent, telling her she was a natural athlete and would be a good baseball player. And it was de León who bought Lefty her first baseball glove.

Unbeknown to Lefty and her teammates, de León was preparing them to play against a North American women's baseball team. While Lefty and the Cuban women were training, the AAGPBL was planning for a 1947 trip to Cuba for spring training. With little time to train or learn the game as it was played by the Northerners, de León and his team worked almost daily. As Lefty remembers it, she trained every day with the Estrellas Cubanas. In May 1947 over two hundred AAGPBL players and league personnel came by train to Miami and from there to Havana. For them the experience was very different from that of previous years, when spring training trips had been notorious for the heat, bad housing accommodations, and long days. In Cuba they were housed at the Saville-Biltmore Hotel and played at the Gran Stadium. It would be a memorable experience.

De León's players and the baseball fans of Havana were enthusiastic about the new arrivals. Lefty does not remember being nervous, but she certainly was excited. She remembers with pride the first game she played against them. Lefty pitched in that game and quips, "I guess I did beautifully." Indeed she did; she did not give up a single hit—and she was still only thirteen. "I don't remember being afraid," Lefty recalls. "It wasn't scary. My mother helped get me this chance to play baseball, and when she told me to play and not give up, I did that. Now I think I would be afraid," she says laughingly.

While Lefty may not remember being afraid to play in that game, it must have been at least a bit nerve-wracking facing that enormous crowd. Harold Dailey, the president of the AAGPBL's South Bend Blue Sox, remembered, "The Americanos became the rage of all baseball-mad Cuba. Hundreds turned out to see them practice. And no less than 50,000 wildly enthusiastic fans watched the round-robin tournament which concluded the training program. In the opening game of the final series between the Racine Belles and the Muskegon Lassies, the crowd numbered over 20,000 and gave convincing proof that Cuba had taken girls' baseball to heart."[13] When asked about the number of fans in the stands for the games, Lefty shrugs it off because it was not that memory she still held; rather it was being on the field with the best.

For the exhibition games the teams were mixed, with both Cuban and North American ballplayers on each team. That meant Lefty got to play alongside one of women's baseball's best players, Dottie Kamenshek—"Kammie"—who played first base on her team. Lefty remembers, "I will never forget looking over there and seeing her. She was the best, you know?" Kamenshek was the league's all-time batting leader. She won two batting titles, with averages of .316 and .306. Also she was a serious base-stealing threat. In 1946 Kamenshek stole 109 bases and finished second only to Sophie Kurys, who stole 201.[14] While Kamenshek had impressive statistics and Lefty knew she was the league's best (and probably best-known) player, it was Kammie's stature, her presence, that awed Lefty: "I looked over there, and I saw this tall woman—I'm short so she was really tall to me—and I thought to myself, 'That lady must be good because she looks like it.'"

Lefty struggled with a lack of confidence her entire life, and she often admired people who were confident and self-assured. Kammie was the epitome of confidence, so it is no wonder that memory, and not the fifty thousand fans or her own stellar performance, that stood out for Lefty decades later. Lefty's determination to make that game about other players—those better known and, in her mind, simply better—is telling. She is a quiet and unassuming individual. In 1947, when she was put on a baseball diamond with the "best of the best" in women's baseball, she had similar "inferiority feelings" to those from her school days. She explains: "I just didn't know why I was there, playing with them; why me? My mother thought I was a good ballplayer, and Mr. de León did too. But I didn't feel that way, especially when I looked over there and saw Kammie. But I did okay, I guess." Both on and off the field Lefty certainly did more than "okay."

After the exhibition game in which Lefty pitched, Rafael de León brought Max Carey, a former Major Leaguer, manager of the Milwaukee Chicks, and president of the AAGPBL, to the Alvarez home. Lefty remembers being there as Carey explained the AAGPBL to her mother, including the chaperon system, the pay, and the rules by which Lefty would have to abide. She would have to return to Cuba each year in the off-season and would be allowed to return to the league only with a signed contract. While those elements of the contract were important to Virtudes, most significant was that she had managed to secure for her daughter a life in the United States. She had negotiated a contract for her thirteen-year-old daughter to play professional baseball in the United States. It was Max Carey who required Lefty to wait until she was fifteen to join the league in the United States, although he allowed her to join other Cuban players and two AAGPBL teams on a tour of Central and South America during the winter and spring of 1948–49.

This tour came about as a result of a new direction in the AAGPBL. At the end of the 1944 season owner Philip K. Wrigley had decided to cut ties with the AAGPBL and agreed to sell the primary ownership to his longtime adviser, Arthur E. Meyerhoff. An advertising executive with the Wrigley Company since 1932 (when Philip's father ran the company), Meyerhoff had been responsible for the publicity and promotion of the league since its inception. Because the two men shared a vision of how the league should be run and especially how it should be represented to the public, the exchange of ownership was easier for both. Between 1944, when he took over the reins of the league, and 1950, when he stepped away, Meyerhoff brought a number of changes, and the result was the league's most successful period. Meyerhoff turned the league into a profit-based venture by expanding its reach and popularity.[15]

Arthur Meyerhoff's management corporation explored several possibilities for expansion, including travel for spring training, exhibition tours, barnstorming teams, winter league opportunities, and the establishment of organizations throughout the country based on the AAGPBL model. Many of the ideas did not survive the planning stage, but some were very successful and became the financial foundation of the league. Initially Meyerhoff's administration focused heavily on tours, which introduced the league to new fans. In May 1945 wartime travel restrictions were still in place, so spring training was held in Chicago, and a preseason exhibition tour was scheduled for military bases within a short distance of Chicago. By the following season Meyerhoff's plan for league expansion and increased publicity was well under way.

Meyerhoff needed new ballplayers every year, but with the league's expansion and despite the recruitment efforts of the touring teams, there never seemed to be enough good talent. While softball players were good athletes and had the skills to play baseball, Meyerhoff realized that it took time to train them. It was hard for some softball players to adjust to the longer base paths and pitching distances. To develop good players the AAGPBL began Junior League Girls Baseball in 1946. Schools did not provide a pool of recruits, so Meyerhoff returned to the playground, from where many of the original players had come in 1943. With Meyerhoff using his influence and with the help of the Chicago Park District and local recreation departments, the junior leagues trained young women in the AAGPBL version of the game. Perhaps the best known of these playground leagues was created by Leonard (Lenny) Zintak. Because of his success with and dedication to women's baseball, Zintak himself was recruited by Max Carey to create an AAGPBL "minor" league. In 1946 Zintak became the AAGPBL's director of schools and try-outs and affiliates of the League.[16] Shortly thereafter the Chicago Girls Baseball League (CGBL) began. The CGBL was considered a level above the junior leaguers, a status that was demonstrated by the contracts the players were required to sign. While both the junior leagues and the CGBL were meant to be a training ground for the AAGPBL, neither provided very many players to the "major league of girl's baseball."[17] Most of the girls who played in the CGBL came from the Chicago parks system teams, and according to one player, Betty Francis, many of those girls "tried out but never made our league."[18] No more than fifteen players moved through the minor league ranks to join the AAGPBL. Some went directly to league teams, while others joined one of two rookie touring teams, the Sallies or the Colleens.

The AAGPBL presence in Cuba, support for Lefty's team, and commitment to the tour of the Southern Hemisphere came directly out of the realization that for the AAGPBL to continue it would need "future talent," increased visibility, and steady profits.[19] Meyerhoff hoped that postseason exhibitions would provide all three to the league. The first full, five-day exhibition tour split six teams into three groups. It hit thirty-two states and five Canadian provinces, which were essential recruiting grounds for league players and fans.[20] After this first tour executives from the AAGPBL and from de León's team planned a tour that was to include two AAGPBL teams and one Cuban team. The AAGPBL teams were the Atlántidas and the Nortenas, named aptly for that trip. The Cuban team was called the Columbianas.[21] They scheduled forty-four games to be played between September and November 1947. Games were to begin in Cuba, then go on to Santo Domingo, Puerto Rico, Venezuela, Panama, and Mexico. The tour was to end in Texas.[22]

Possibly due to a lack of funds, however, the exhibition never made it out of Cuba. In a letter to players explaining the tour's cancellation, Max Carey wrote in part, "I feel that all of us have been enriched through our experiences in Cuba and it is my hope that future developments in South and Central American countries will again offer us opportunities for the building and extension of Girls Baseball."[23]

The tour for which Lefty signed up did happen, however. Fortunately for her Meyerhoff and Carey were not willing to give up on Latin America as an expansion location for women's baseball. In what was to be a smaller version of the canceled tour, several AAGPBL players and two teams from the Latin American Feminine Béisbol League (LAFBL) gathered in January 1948 to play exhibition games in Maracaibo and Caracas, Venezuela. They played nine games in all, and each brought in an average of seven thousand fans. One game, between combined North American and Latin American players and a team of Venezuelan girls, drew nearly twelve thousand people.[24] Just six weeks after this winter exhibition tour many of the same AAGPBL players rejoined the Cuban players for another tour in Cuba and Puerto Rico. Lefty was part of this tour but has few memories of it.

Lefty's big tour was yet to come. From January through March 1949 Carey and Meyerhoff teamed up for a more ambitious tour. Some of Lefty's most vivid memories of playing ball for Cuba come from her time on this tour. Two AAGPBL teams and a group of Cuban players played games in Guatemala, Nicaragua, Costa Rica, Panama, Venezuela, and Puerto Rico.[25] During this tour the two teams from the AAGPBL were called the Americanas and the

Cuban teams, the Cubanas. Only AAGPBL players played on the Americanas teams, but in order to equalize the talent, some of the North Americans were moved to the Cuban teams.[26] For this tour players from the AAGPBL were paid at least fifty dollars a week, more if "earnings warrant[ed]." Their meals, transportation, and housing were paid by the league, and series winners were promised a bonus.[27] We have no information about the earnings of the Cuban players. It is clear, however, that like the AAGPBL players, they were provided with meals, transportation, and housing.

Lefty does not remember what she was paid for the exhibition tour or whether she was paid at all. "It didn't matter," she says. "That was my first real taste of playing with those girls. And I rode on a plane. Holy cow! . . . I just had to get on the plane. I don't know if my mother was sad or happy. She told me to go, so I did." There is no doubt that Lefty was scared the day she flew. She remembers the fear when the plane took off: "I had never done that before, you know, take a plane. Wow, what was I getting into?" That plane ride took Lefty away from Virtudes's control, out of her own comfort zone, and into the beginning of a very different life.

On January 26, 1949, the teams arrived in Guatemala, where they spent the first four days of the tour. Lefty was young and inexperienced and had not traveled much beyond her neighborhood in Havana, so when they arrived in Guatemala, she struggled to take it all in: "It's funny. I do not have many memories of Guatemala. We were not there long, and I don't know; maybe I was a little nervous." It may have been nervousness and it may have been the shortness of their stay there, but Guatemala did not stand out for her. Lefty's first clear memories of the tour were of the nine-day stop in the baseball-crazed country of Nicaragua.

To Nicaraguans baseball was "*el deporte rey*," the king of sports.[28] Despite any difficulties the Nicaraguan and U.S. governments had, baseball, North America's favorite pastime, was "*el gran juego yanqui*" (the great Yankee game) in Nicaragua. Dating back to the late nineteenth century and continuing through the occupation, dictatorship, revolution, and war of the twentieth century—much as in Cuba—baseball had been a nexus for political conflict in Nicaragua. In his book on Nicaraguan culture Pablo Antonio Cuadras asks why baseball is so popular in Nicaragua when most of its Latin American neighbors prefer soccer. He first suggests that Nicaraguans might simply have been influenced by the country's warm climate to prefer baseball because it requires little energy. He eventually sees a deeper connection between the essence of the game of baseball and the nature of the Nicaraguan soul.[29] "In baseball, personal play stands out," Cuadras writes, "and we are more friends of strong individuals . . . than of cooperative effort." In baseball, as in politics, Nicaraguans are won over by the cult of personality—a big hitter, a big pitcher, or a base stealer.[30]

As in Cuba, baseball fans were able to separate their love for "America's Game" from political tensions with their northern neighbor. And no Nicaraguan was a bigger baseball fan than the country's president, Anastacio Somoza García. While in Nicaragua, the Cuban and AAGPBL players were guests of the Nicaraguan president, and that is a memory Lefty is not likely to forget. On February 1, 1949, the players visited the palace of General Somoza. "He [Somoza] was charming," says Lefty. "We all had to dress up. There was very good food and dancing. Some of them danced, but I did not want to. But then General Somoza asked me to dance, and I had to do it. He asked if I wanted to stay in Nicaragua with him. I said no. I was so scared, but I do not think he meant it."[31] Or perhaps he did. As the players were leaving the palace, Somoza's son took the hand of one of the AAG-PBL players, Annabelle Lee Harmon, and said (as she recalls it), "If there is anything I can do to you, let me know." Not only did Somoza host the players, but he also threw out the first pitch to begin the game between the Cuban and North American teams. His picture appeared on the front page of the local newspaper, and the caption read, "General Anastacio Somoza, Minister of Defense, threw out the first ball in the game between the Cuban and North American teams the day before yesterday in the afternoon."[32]

It seems that AAGPBL league officials were excited about and more than willing to use Somoza's participation and support of the women to their advantage, despite his reputation as a brutal dictator. In a press release dated February 10, 1949, the league called the players "America's newest good-will ambassadors to the Latin Americas." It adds that they were so good at their jobs that the Nicaraguan minister of defense "publicly stated that he intends to import a Yankee manager to teach young women of his country how to play the game." Finally, the press release claims that Somoza witnessed all the games and called himself "one of the games' newest and most enthusiastic fans."[33] For Lefty neither the politics, nor Somoza himself mattered: "I did not care about that dictator. Maybe I feel different now that I am older, but I did not care about him then." She was just as happy to move on from Managua to smaller towns and then to other countries. From Managua the players traveled to the town of León.

One of the AAGPBL players, Ruth Richard, kept a diary during the tour and wrote of the trip from Managua to León: "We rode the bullet train thru dirt streets, saw one storied bldgs.—homes, farms, towns, and transportation very crude." As for the players' housing arrangements, she wrote: "There were two rooms upstairs [in the hotel] with cots in them—we used the larger one to undress in. No running water—only a pitcher, a basin, and a towel for 32 girls. Who wants to wash anyway?" It seems that the playing conditions were not much better than the accommodations in León. Richard remembers that they "played ball in the dust bowl. Stands were small and made of hardened clay. Seats were folding chairs—roof was tin."[34] Despite the somewhat difficult playing conditions, games were well attended, and for Lefty they were not that different from the way she was used to playing the game of baseball. It was not the conditions that bothered her; instead it was the travel itself that frightened her.

Despite Lefty's insistence that she has few memories of that first flight from Havana to Guatemala, the issue of travel and the anxiety it caused her continue to be a constant part of her memories of the tour. Most travel was via airplane, except when the teams were traveling within countries; then trains were used. Planes were small, and many of the players reported being nervous as they boarded them. "Some of the girls rode in the cockpit," Lefty says, "but not me. I was not that brave." Despite the fear Lefty felt while traveling, she also remembers the sights: "We flew over beautiful mountains and rivers, through clouds; I will never forget how the world looked from up there. I was scared most of the time, but, oh, the sights!" Despite her fear and anxiety about travel, Lefty stayed with the tour through its end.

From Nicaragua the teams went to Costa Rica. There they were honored by the U.S. ambassador and his wife, who attended their game at the National

Soccer Stadium. From there they traveled to Balboa, Panama, where they had a very busy schedule. In one day they rode fifty miles, played a game in Mt. Hope Stadium, and, despite being exhausted, spent time at the Panama Canal. After touring the canal, they went "back to the barracks, supper and another ball game. Mickey (Migdalia Perez) hurled for the Cubans and Beans (Earlene Risinger) for the Americans. Game was good and so was crowd."[35]

After Panama they played games in Caracas, Venezuela, where, compared to the fields on which they had been playing, the diamonds were "in good shape and well kept." According to Ruth Richard, "The crowds were large (three to one male) and very enthusiastic and especially interested in blonde players."[36] The experience of playing on well-kept fields and in front of large crowds was both exciting and difficult for Lefty. "I love the field," she says. "But it was big, the crowd. And loud. I don't know; maybe I was nervous." The Central and South American tour was to wrap up in Santo Domingo, Dominican Republic, and finally Cuba. There is no evidence that games were played, however. Lefty remembers playing in the other locations but not in these. Indeed many of Lefty's memories of this tour are vague, but she is very clear about the real importance of the trip: "Making those first American friends was the best thing. I would never have known them or seen the Panama Canal. I loved that." Despite her fear of travel and her insecurities as a ballplayer, the Latin American tour was a success for Lefty. It provided her with some self-confidence and a foundation on which her professional baseball career could be built.

Once back in Cuba, Lefty returned to her home in El Cerro. Under the watchful eye of her mother she spent the next two months preparing for her departure to the United States and the beginning of her professional baseball career. It was a stressful time. Lefty remembers: "My mother watched me always. I could not go out, could not date or even be out of my mother's sight for too long. She was afraid that people would take advantage of me because they knew I was going to the U.S." Lefty does not remember family or friends stopping by to say goodbye or wish her good luck. In fact, she has the distinct impression that her mother did not want a lot of people to know about her departure: "I think because she was not treated right, [my mother] did not trust people and wanted me to have this chance. She couldn't go but I could, and she did not want anything to get in my way." It is likely that Virtudes's controlling behavior stemmed from fear. She had worked for years to find Lefty a way out of poverty and a path out of Cuba. They were close to realizing that dream, and she did not want to leave anything to chance.

While Virtudes may have had good reason to protect Lefty in this manner, the isolation was hard for Lefty and made it difficult for her to socialize once she was on her own. "I just didn't know how to do it," she claims. "I was nervous and unsure. I just never knew how to talk to people, like tell them what I wanted or how I felt." Whether due to shyness, fear, or insecurity, Lefty had not found her voice by the time she left Cuba for the United States; that fact, combined with her lack of English, made for a very difficult transition.

Lefty's preparation for the move to the United States was hampered because she did not speak English: "I did not know much English; my mother was tutoring me with words. There was a professor in Cuba, a neighbor; he was supposed to teach me English, and my mother sent me to him for a week. She thought I could learn English in a week. I did not know much English in a week." From language to social expectations Lefty was simply not ready for the challenges that lay ahead for her, and she alone knew that to be true.

Yet in May 1949 Lefty did not voice her fears or uncertainties when she went with her family to the Havana airport. Rather, she says, "I picked up my bag and walked up those steps to a new life." When asked if she was afraid that day, she says, "No. I was not sure if my mother was crying or not. I didn't look back. I just walked up those steps to the plane. She wanted this for me and told me to do it, so I did. No questions." Lefty does not have any memory of her father's or brother's last words to her, only her mother's: "Remember, you are a ballplayer. Never give up. You are a ballplayer." It was with her mother's confidence, the glove given to her by de León, a borrowed suitcase, and the naiveté of a fifteen-year-old that Lefty boarded that plane to the United States.

CHAPTER FOUR

Coming to America

It is what my mother always wanted for me. Life in America.

LEFTY ALVAREZ

With wide eyes and a shake of her head Lefty recalled just how amazing it was to be on her way to the United States in 1949: "It was funny how fast it all happened. My mother said I should play baseball because I was good and because it would help me out of Cuba. I did not know I wanted to be out of Cuba, but she thought it better for me if I was. So I played, and the next thing I know, she is packing for me to go to America. Holy cow, America!" Baseball was both a way out of Cuba for Lefty and a much-needed anchor for her once she arrived in the United States. She was completely unprepared for the different customs, food, music, and especially the language she encountered. Nothing was like what Lefty had known, and because she spoke very little English, America was often difficult for her to navigate or understand: "The first time I stepped here in the United States was to go play for . . . it was Chicago. And coming fresh from Cuba at that age, I didn't even know I was in Chicago." Lefty's knowledge of the United States was limited, and she simply did not know what to expect. Fortunately Lefty's teammates provided a network of people she both liked and trusted. She was going to need them. The monumental changes to Lefty's life were only just beginning.

Lefty's travel from Cuba to Chicago was, according to her, "no big deal." Once she arrived in Chicago, however, "The deal got big. . . . I will never forget arriving in Chicago that first time. I could not believe the buildings. We never had anything like that in Cuba." Chicago in the 1940s was a city flush with people and industry. During World War II Chicago produced more steel than the United Kingdom every year from 1939 to 1945 and more than Nazi Germany from 1943 to 1945. The city was second only to Detroit in the value of war goods produced.[1] By the time Lefty arrived, Chicago was a bustling city with large skyscrapers and more people than she had ever seen. Its population was 3,620,962—much larger than the roughly 1.5 million people who lived in Havana.[2] Lefty remembers: "From that first day I thought to myself, 'Where did all these people come from, and where are they going?'"

Lefty's initial trip to the United States was made a bit easier because she knew that other Cuban woman had already traveled there to play ball. After the AAGPBL had its spring training trip in Havana in 1947, Cuban women signed contracts to play in the North American league. Eulalia Gonzales was the first of the Cuban women to play in the league, with the 1947 Racine Belles, before returning home to Cuba. Georgiana Ríos, another early signee, played only during the 1948 season. Mirtha Marrero, Luisa Gallegos, Migdalia "Mickey" Pérez, Gloria Ruiz, and Zonia Vialat all played in the AAGPBL during the 1948 season.[3]

For the four Cuban women in the league who stayed the longest—Marrero, Pérez, Lefty, and Ysora "Chico" Castillo—their lives changed drastically. Marrero and Pérez played for the Chicago Colleens in 1948. They were the only two Cuban women on the team that year, and both were happy in 1949, when Lefty and Castillo joined the team. Lefty traveled from Cuba with the three other Colleens, which, she says, "made my trip less scary and those first days in Chicago easier." She continued to rely on those women throughout her career. She remains fond of them, recognizing that without them her time in the AAGPBL and the United States might also have been very short.

For all the Cubans the most difficult challenge was the language barrier. Mirtha Marrero admitted to Jane Moffet, her teammate, just how hard it was to be the only Spanish-speaking player on her team. Jane recalls Mirtha saying, "I cried a lot because the American girls couldn't understand, me and I couldn't understand them. I had a hard time." That isolation changed when Pérez joined the Colleens, followed by Lefty and Castillo. Even though Lefty joined a team that already had Cuban players, the transition was at times excruciating for her. Struggling to fit in and trying to focus on baseball made for a very difficult beginning to Lefty's life in the United States: "I had a hard time when we met the American girls. I did not speak English, so I just didn't try to talk to them." Like in Marrero's case, some of Lefty's most painful memories are of those early years in the United States, when situations arose because of her inability to comprehend or speak English.

Often teammates or players from other teams teased Lefty or made fun of her attempts to engage in conversation. Outwardly Lefty laughed at the jokes, even though she neither fully understood nor appreciated being the brunt of them. Inside she suffered and pushed herself more deeply inward: "It made me feel more alone when I didn't understand, but I think they did not mean to hurt me, so I just did not speak up. It was hard sometimes." Lefty differentiated between what she called "bad fun" and "good fun." She seemed to distinguish between those who were intentionally trying to hurt her and those who liked her but wanted only to be playful. Either way, the teasing took a toll on her. The pressure of living her mother's dream in America was a heavy burden for Lefty and often kept her from talking to friends about how lonely she was or how deeply the teasing hurt her. She says, "My mother gave me this chance, and even when it was hard, she said I should not complain. So I didn't."

While the language barrier made it hard to communicate, the cultural, social, and even culinary differences made nearly everything more difficult. Mary "Wimp" Baumgartner remembers arriving in Chicago for the same tryouts that brought Lefty to the city. Wimp was very intrigued by the Cubans: "They brought in four Cubans, and Lefty Alvarez was one of those Cubans; of course none of them could talk English or anything. All they did was eat scrambled eggs and hamburgers and I don't know what they drank, but that's all they ate. I think that's all they knew how to order."[4] Lefty's memory of ordering food confirms Wimp's assessment: "All I knew how to order was hamburger. . . . I learned to say that, and so that was all I ate." Despite these cultural differences and the language barrier, Lefty and the other Cuban players managed to adjust to life outside Cuba, but the loneliness for Lefty did not start to recede until she began to live the life of a baseball player.

For the first two years of her contract Lefty played with the Chicago

Colleens, which was a touring team. Touring teams were made up of girls who were young and less experienced, and for Lefty that was a good thing. For some players, however, playing on the touring teams was a disappointment. They were usually a bit older than Lefty (who was only fifteen), and for them it was akin to being assigned to the Minor Leagues and meant that they were not yet good enough to play in the Majors. For Lefty, however, the Colleens provided the sense of family and security she desperately needed. "I left family for family," she says. Being a Chicago Colleen, playing with younger girls, and traveling the United States to be in somewhat less stressful exhibition games was the perfect beginning to Lefty's life in the league.

Of course for those who played on the touring teams, their job was to travel. Both the Chicago Colleens and the league's other touring team, the Springfield Sallies, spent a lot of time on the road. "I always sat in the front of the bus," Lefty says. "I tried to read the road signs to see where we were and to try and learn English. The other girls made fun of me, but not bad fun, good fun."[5] Despite the teasing and pranks they pulled on her, Lefty was close to the other players and relied on their friendship. Baseball was a common language between Lefty and her teammates, and through the game she was able to connect to people, learn English, and develop lifelong friendships.[6] In fact, when asked to recall her days as a Colleen, Lefty does not start spouting her statistics. She does not recite her greatest accomplishments on the baseball diamond, nor does she remember her longest hit or the best-pitched game. Rather, "It was the relationships that were most important," she says. "I was not always a happy person back then and did not feel good enough on the field. It was hard to understand the language, so I felt I missed a lot from the coaches. On the field I did not feel very good sometimes. But I had good friends, and they helped me."[7] Lefty's baseball statistics show she struggled on the field early on. No statistics were kept for 1949. In 1950 she hit .256, and her pitching record was 6-6.[8] Given her insecurities, however, it is not likely that she would have felt any better about her play had the numbers been higher. Having the close connections with her teammates was always important to her, and that did not change throughout her life.

Lefty's ability to survive the loneliness and the pranks took strength and courage she did not even realize she had. When asked about the harsh pranks and how she managed to forgive the other players, Lefty replies, "Well, whenever I had hard times, in ball or before [I started playing], I thought about other things—you know, things, places where I was okay. Good at something. A place that was safe, where I knew I was strong. That was always in a sport. Usually baseball, but sometimes not. I was just good there, and I remembered it. Then I held my head up. Funny, isn't it, how sports can do that for you?" Despite the teasing Lefty was able to see the good in her teammates: "My teammates made fun of me sometimes and played jokes on me, but they also looked out for me. I was lucky I had them, that I still have them." However, her teammates did not always take care of her. As a young girl who was struggling with the language and with understanding the customs, she was also vulnerable. Most incidents in which Lefty was taken advantage were minor. Someone took her place in line or on the bus, or the players manipulated her into paying for a meal. One incident was not minor at all, and it still causes great confusion and shame for Lefty.

The incident involved a player-manager and chaperone for the Springfield Sallies, Barbara "Bobbie" Liebrich. Liebrich was highly respected and had a wide-ranging career with the AAGPBL. She played for Rockford and Kenosha in 1948 and was hired to be the player-manager and chaperone of the Springfield Sallies in 1949 and 1950. In 1953 she would become the chaperone for the Kalamazoo Lassies. In 1949 Lefty's first year with the AAGPBL, Liebrich approached Lefty and asked her for a favor. Lefty remembers: "She told me her job was in jeopardy if the Sallies didn't get a win. I did not know how all that works and was always told to do as superiors tell you."[9] Liebrich pleaded with Lefty, who was scheduled to pitch for the Colleens the next day, to lose her upcoming game so that Liebrich could stay in the league. Much to Lefty's chagrin, she agreed, reminiscing, "She was selfish, I had no thought about my future or what this would do for me and I was too young, 15 at the time, and too scared to realize it myself."[10] Unsure how she lost that game or even if she did it on purpose or not, Lefty just remembers the hug from Liebrich after the game: "She came to me and gave me a big hug after the game. I did not hug back, just stood there. Why did she do that?"[11] There is no way to verify this story with Liebrich, who died in July 2006, but this was Lefty's memory. Even if the years have dulled the edges of the story, it is her story to tell. She did not tell anyone about the incident and sadly carried the guilt for nearly sixty years.

Naturally not everyone took advantage of Lefty's youth. Despite the difficulties discussed above, Lefty claims she had fun: "In those years, I played baseball so I could be here and have fun. It was not for the love of baseball."[12] "Fun" to Lefty meant freedom from her mother in Cuba, a chance to learn and grow on her own, and an opportunity to see more of the world than her mother had ever thought possible. "My mother wanted me to come to America," she says, "but she didn't know what that meant—that I would be here learning new things, being different than I could ever be there." While it is hard to know exactly what "being different than [she] could be there" means, if we recall Lefty's stories about the ways in which her mother controlled every minute of her life, it is possible to imagine that a chance to make her own decisions and friendships was akin to a declaration of independence for her. That independence was short lived.

Because the AAGPBL's yearly contracts stated that each of the foreign players had to go home after the season, at the end of each season from 1949 to 1953 Lefty returned to Cuba and lived under the watchful eye of her mother. She did not work, go out much, or date. Virtudes was perhaps even more protective of Lefty during those off-season trips home. Lefty understood that her mother "was trying to keep me safe from harm from neighbors or potential boyfriends," but the seclusion was hard. Virtudes allowed some people to come to the house, Lefty remembers. "It was like they were there to view me, like I was a doll or something. I think my mother wanted people to see how well I was doing, that I was successful."

Lefty received letters from teammates in the United States, and this made Virtudes as happy as it did Lefty. For Virtudes, Lefty's off-season connection to the United States was crucial in maintaining a level of prestige in the neighborhood. It also reassured Virtudes that Lefty was doing well in America, making friends, and adjusting to the cultural changes. If all these people were her friends and wanted to keep in touch with her, Lefty must be successfully making the transition from a poor, unknown Cuban girl to a well-known, well-liked, professional U.S. baseball player. Lefty, on the other hand, was happy to hear from friends but was never as concerned about success as her mother. For her those letters represented friendships with and connections to people and not to her status as a professional athlete. In fact, she says, "These letters didn't matter to me in the same way. To be a professional baseball player was good, but mostly baseball was the reason I had chances." The opportunity to make friends, something she rarely had the chance to do in Cuba, and the chance to create, for herself, a "good life in America" was what both the league and those letters represented to Lefty.

In 1950 Lefty returned to the United States for her second season with the Chicago Colleens. She was a bit older and had some idea what to expect, so her second year was much easier than her first. Still language and cultural barriers remained a problem. Lefty gives an example:

> The other girls continued to tease me because I still struggled with the language. We had to eat in restaurants a lot, and the only words I knew were "hamburger" and "chocolate milkshake." Whenever we went to a restaurant, that's all I ordered. I don't know for how long, but I couldn't say anything else. They laughed at me, but I didn't care. I got hamburgers and chocolate milkshakes! One time, though, I got confused. The menu said scrambled eggs with jam and toast and coffee and potatoes. So when I got my order, I said, "Where is the ham?" "Ham" is spelled "jamon" in Spanish, so I thought "jam" must be "ham."[13]

It was in the 1950 season that Lefty began to develop the friendships that sustain her to this day. Perhaps her best friend in the league—and the woman to whom years later she still referred as her "counselor—was Jane Moffet. Moffet, also a rookie in 1949, played with the Springfield Sallies in 1949 and 1950. Since the two rookie teams, the Colleens and the Sallies, traveled together, Jane and Lefty often roomed together. It is interesting that, like Lefty, Jane also owed her presence in the league to the intervention of someone else. Jane made the league without having first seriously considered it. In 1949 she was a freshman at East Stroudsburg University of Pennsylvania when a friend told her about the AAGPBL tryouts in Allentown. The classmate did not want to go alone, so she convinced Moffet to go along. Moffet, who was a good athlete but had never been a baseball player, offered her assistance to league executive Lenny Zintak and was soon fielding balls and helping out with the tryouts. Zintak, the league advance man in charge of player development for the AAGPBL, asked her to try out. Moffet, not her classmate, left with a contract in her hand. She was assigned to the Springfield Sallies and then to the Chicago Colleens to gain more experience.

Moffet certainly gained baseball experience, but the experiences she most remembers happened as a result of her housing assignment. For reasons she does not know, while she was playing for the Colleens she was assigned to room with the Cubans: Mirtha Marrero, Luisa Gallegos, Migdalia Pérez, Georgiana Ríos, Gloria Ruiz, and Lefty Alvarez. Reflecting on this experience, Jane says, "I will never forget walking into the room for the first time. There were clothes hanging everywhere, wet ones and dry ones, everywhere." She did not immediately realize that the Cuban girls did not speak English, so when she asked, "What the hell is going on?" they did not respond. So she took matters into her own hands. "I didn't understand them, and they did not understand me, so I just reached up and pulled the clothes down that were hanging over the empty bed. [Then] I think they understood." Mickey Pérez and Jane became friends first. Because Lefty was younger and because Mickey was tasked with watching out for her, Jane was drafted by Mickey into a "lifelong effort to keep Lefty out of trouble." Throughout their time together in the league Lefty relied on Jane for friendship, understanding, and guidance.

Moffet readily recalls incidents when Lefty suffered at the hands of the other girls: "I remember one time some of the girls took a couple of row boats out on a lake. They put Lefty in one; then, when they got to the middle, they took her paddles and left her to find her way back to shore." In another incident Lefty was lost in New York City because the girls "just went off and left her. They thought it was funny, I think." Lefty remembers that time as hard, sometimes painful and lonely, but she remembers it with a smile: "I know they liked me," she says. "They just teased me because I did not understand them, and I was young."

For players on the Sallies and the Colleens the 1950 barnstorming season was special because it included exhibition games in New England and the northeastern part of the United States. The highlight included a three-inning exhibition game at Yankee Stadium. "We shared a lot that year" Lefty says. "Lots of hard times for me anyway, but also great things. Like Yankee stadium, wow!" Prior to a Yankees game with the Philadelphia Athletics, the Sallies and the Colleens played in a game that became one of their most exciting memories of the tour. The Colleens played out of the Philadelphia dugout and the Sallies out of the Yankee dugout. Jane Moffet was one of those for whom the game in Yankee Stadium was so significant. She was not a Yankee fan, and the idea of playing in Yankee Stadium was initially not even that big of a deal for her, but that quickly changed:

> The Yankees had completed their infield play and came back to the dugout. I was preparing to warm up our pitcher and found myself in the dugout with several of the Yankee ball players. I was with Yogi, Whitey Ford, Casey Stengel, and others. Casey and Yogi were very friendly and stayed with us in the dugout talking baseball. I went out and warmed up the pitcher, and we played our three-inning game. Then we stayed for the game. I have been a devoted Yankee fan ever since. All in the life of a rookie.

While Lefty too remembers the trip to Yankee Stadium, she also recalls an incident that happened off the field. Lefty and Mirtha went off to do some sightseeing. Never having been in a city the size of New York, they were overwhelmed by the people, traffic, and "ways of the road." After roaming around the city for hours, they realized they were lost. Since they had very little money and spoke even less English, they decided to walk rather than get a taxi. As they searched for their hotel, a police officer stopped them crossing a busy street. He nearly arrested Lefty for jaywalking. As he tried, with little success, to explain what "jaywalking" was, both women looked confused and responded only in Spanish. Finally says Lefty, the officer "gave up in frustration, I think. I tried to tell him I did not know the ways of the road, but he did not want to hear." In fact, Mirtha could speak some English but had told Lefty to address the officer in Spanish only. Fortunately they were not arrested and did eventually find their way back to the team hotel. Lefty emphasizes, "I was never really afraid [because] I just jumped into things, new things, and was never afraid. Even in that big city. What was I thinking?" Whether it was finding her way back to shore without a paddle, nearly getting arrested, or simply handling constant teasing and practical jokes, Lefty managed to see such incidents as a sign of love and acceptance by her teammates. Being a part of the team, even if that meant enduring the teasing of a few, was important to Lefty.

So was playing baseball and being part of the AAGPBL's barnstorming tour. Lefty and the other players understood that the league need to sell itself around the country, and they were on the front lines of that effort. By all accounts the 1950 barnstorming tour was very successful. The game at Yankee Stadium was televised, and a number of young women called the league offices seeking information about tryouts.[14] In addition, because of the positive reaction from fans after the televised game, plans were made to televise a game scheduled to be played in Rochester, New York, later that year.[15] And Lefty was a perfect example of how those tours helped to create stronger, more independent baseball players. Lefty learned from incidents such as her and Mirtha's near arrest in New York to help her gain the courage and confidence to continue. The league did not keep statistics for the touring teams in 1950, but Lefty believes that she progressed in her play that year and was ready for the "big leagues." She would have to wait until she got her contract that winter to find out where she would be playing in 1951.

As successful as the AAGPBL exhibition tours were, the league decided not to continue them after the 1950 season. This decision made it harder to find and recruit new talent. By the 1950s the league's brand of baseball had changed from a version of the game that employed many of the same skills used by softballers to a stricter form of baseball. This made it much more difficult to train softball players for the league than it had been. As Meyerhoff had realized many years before, softball players needed a great deal of training and experience if they were to be successful in the AAGPBL. With recruiting increasingly difficult, some of the players feared for the future of the league with the cancellation of the tours. Many players were aware that the league had been struggling during 1950–1951. Some players either left the league for other baseball or softball leagues or simply played each season knowing it might be the last.

To make matters worse, league administration changed drastically in 1950, resulting in a number of operational changes, many of which likely hastened the league's demise. At the end of the 1950 season Arthur Meyerhoff and his management corporation ended their connection to the league. In December 1950 Meyerhoff sold the rights of the league to his board of directors, and the AAGPBL was dissolved and reorganized under a new administration.[16] Owners began to operate their teams independently. Without a centralized body to control publicity, promotion, player recruitment, and player training, the league began a downward slide. Financial problems, declining fan attendance, and a lack of centralized focus, combined with an increase in televised baseball games, made the continuation of the league nearly impossible. The image of the league that had flourished during Meyerhoff's tenure faltered throughout the country. National coverage of the league's competitive play remained, but because the budgets for promotion and advertising of the entire league were almost nonexistent and the financial burden fell to the individual teams, national publicity ceased.

Unaware of this growing crisis, after her second year Lefty again returned home to Cuba for the off-season. "It was so hard for me," she says. "I was not a happy kid for all kinds of reasons, and when I went back to Cuba in the off-season, it was like going back to that unhappy place." Alone and with no control over her life, Lefty went "into her head" and remembered the times when she was happy. "I thought about my friends in America," she says. "They did not always understand me either, but at least it was only my language they were confused about and not my whole self." Clearly Virtudes did not know her daughter at that point and could not possibly understand how Lefty's life differed from what she had expected it to be.

Neither Lefty nor Virtudes could have imagined just how Lefty would change or how the separation from her family would take her away from them so completely. Once she spent time in the United States and tasted a bit of the freedom that living apart from her family provided, even returning to Cuba for the off-season was hard for Lefty. She reflects: "I did not want to go back, be there with all the troubles going on in my family. It was hard each time, and every time I went back, I was less happy to be there." It must have been very much like a young woman's going off to college and having to return home to live with her parents for the summer. The relationship between that young woman and her parents could never be the same, regardless of how much the parents tried to impose their will. A child who has experienced independence rarely accepts parental control again without a fight. Lefty sums up: "I went back. I survived. My body was in Cuba, but my mind was playing ball in America."

For Lefty playing baseball was both fun and a struggle, as interviews with her indicate. She went back and forth between talking about how hard it was to play in the AAGPBL, how she struggled to understand the coaches, and how much fun it was to be part of that league. But whether she is retelling a fond memory or a difficult one, singing the praises of the league, or remembering the loneliness she experienced while playing in the United States, the part of her identity that protects, fights back, and ultimately wins out is the part informed by sport. She recalls: "Sometimes while I was in Cuba, sitting, doing nothing, I would think I was playing ball, my sport a part of me, and I would feel better." Lefty may not have realized it at the time, but it was more than just reliving happy memories of playing baseball or reconnecting to the sport part of herself that helped her survive the return to Cuba. Those memories represent her reliance on sport and the impact it had on her life. Sport always provided the foundation of Lefty's identity, the location where strength, courage, and confidence were created. The memory of a time when only sport and her connection to it would ground her, make her feel better, more confident, and, in her own words, "worthy of my mother's praise," illustrates this fact. Lefty had no way of knowing then, but she would have to rely on that "sport part of herself" many times during her career.

While in Cuba before the 1951 season, Lefty got a new contract, and this time she was told to report to the Fort Wayne Daisies. In the context of the AAGPBL, this was the big leagues! Mirtha Marrero would be her teammate. This promotion was a source of great pride for Lefty's mother, but for Lefty it created a new anxiety: "I was proud too but did not want to leave the Colleens. They were my friends. I was comfortable there, and I was nervous about how I would do in Fort Wayne. Not so nervous I did not want to do it, but just scared I would mess up." As she had done in 1949, when she had left Cuba for the first time, Lefty got on the plane to Miami and never looked back. "I was scared," she confesses, "but my mother was proud, so I was too. At least I would get to play baseball, and that is when I am happy, so I went."

Mirtha and Lefty were met at the Miami airport by Max Carey, likely the best known of the league's managers. He had been hired in 1944 to manage the Milwaukee Chicks and had won the pennant that season; he was also hired to serve as the league's president through 1950. Lefty remembers that Carey was known to take a friendly but firm approach to his players. "Max met us at the Miami airport," Lefty says. He drove us to Fort Wayne. Holy Cow! From Miami to Fort Wayne. Mirtha and I both rode in the front seat with him all the way, Mirtha sitting in the middle. Max flirted with her, laughing; he was having a good time riding with us." During the drive Carey spelled out the names of towns for them, talked baseball, and tried to make them feel comfortable. He no doubt worried that the transition would be a difficult one for both Lefty and Mirtha.

Lefty envied Mirtha, who, according to Lefty, was more outgoing and made friends more quickly than she did. Because she spoke some English, Mirtha could more easily figure out what the coaches wanted. Unlike Mirtha, Lefty just "felt inferior to the players" she was about to join, so the move was difficult and scary. This insecurity was not only about being around new people, being in a new place, or having to make new friends; it was also about her playing ability. While Lefty was becoming a good baseball player, she was not developing the way the league probably had hoped. The league's disappointment likely has more to do with her inability to take instruction from the coaches than her athletic talent, but the fact remained that in 1951, when she began her career with the Daisies, she was not among the best—a fact she knew all too well.

Lefty did eventually make a lot of friends in Fort Wayne. In fact from her first days in Indiana, Lefty was accepted and cared for by a host family named the Finfrocks. Lefty describes them:

My biggest thrill in coming to the U.S. was in 1951 coming to Fort Wayne and [meeting] some real Daisy fans. The Finfrocks were waiting for me with a winter coat. It was still a little cool, and they knew I was coming from a warm country. For me it was unforgettable how they thought about it. I roomed in their house for a short time until the league found another place for me to stay. Why they were there to pick me up, I do not exactly know, except they were real Daisy fans. With me I had a piece a paper my mother had written for me to give to the Finfrocks. She wrote it in English in her own handwriting: "I am glad to be back in this wonderful country." She did not know English, but she found a way to write it. To me this is [a] very important [indication] of her wisdom and the respect she had for this country. [It is] one of the reasons I did get adjusted very well, and from day one I liked Fort Wayne.

On the field, however, Lefty struggled. Playing for Fort Wayne was not easy for her. Still only seventeen and struggling to communicate, she did not stand out among the more experienced U.S. players. Again the language barrier made it hard for Lefty to understand the coaches, and her inability to understand led to a lack of aggressiveness on her part. Lefty remembered that during batting practice she would just stand back and wait while the others stepped up to the plate repeatedly. She often did not get to bat, she says, because she just "hung back and did not assert" herself. Obviously if she didn't practice, she was not going to improve. In fact her hitting suffered: "Since I was a pitcher, people thought I didn't need to hit well, but I felt bad that I was not good at that part of the game."

In hindsight Lefty is most upset that she was not living up to her potential or her mother's expectations. She was angry that she did not speak up for herself, play more aggressively, or learn the game better. Baseball is a game of statistics, and Lefty's batting averages illustrate her struggle better than words. In 1950, as noted, she hit .256, but in 1951 she hit only .095.[17] Lefty's pitching totals are equally telling. In 1950 she pitched in thirteen games, won six, lost six, and had one no decision. In 1951 she also played in thirteen games but won only two of them. The other eleven games were no decisions. Fortunately for Lefty her play improved in subsequent years, but the comparison between her 1950 season and her first year in the "big leagues" is a good indication of just how much she struggled.

Although Lefty began the 1951 season in Fort Wayne, she was sent to Michigan to play for the Battle Creek Belles partway through. Battle Creek had suffered several injuries that year, and players from other teams were sent to bolster the team. South Bend Blue Sox pitcher Sue Kidd remembered that her team had a full roster of pitchers, and since Battle Creek was struggling, she was loaned to them.[18] Since both she and Lefty had been loaned to the team temporarily, they became close friends. Like Kidd, Lefty spent only part of the 1951 season in Battle Creek. The Belles finished last in the first half of the 1951 season, 11-45. After being strengthened by Lefty, Kidd, and others, they improved to 19-35 in the second half of the season for an overall record 30-80. Lefty has few memories of her time in Battle Creek; in fact she did not even mention that she played there when we first talked about her playing career. She was not there long enough for it to feel like home in the way that Fort Wayne did. As was required of her after every season, Lefty returned to Cuba when the 1951 season ended.

Back in Cuba Lefty anxiously waited, as she did every off-season, for her 1952 contract. The arrival of the next year's contract was an important event for both Lefty and her mother, and much of the summer was spent in anticipation of its appearance in the mailbox. That contract meant she could continue to play baseball for the AAGPBL, but most important, it allowed her to return to the United States. Immigration required the contract paperwork before Lefty and the other Cuban players would be allowed to reenter the United States. In 1952 Mirtha Marrero, Ysora Castillo, and Mickey Pérez received contracts in the off-season, but Lefty's did not arrive. Lefty had been certain that she would be invited back to play in the league, but when her contract did not arrive, she remembered feeling ambivalent: "I knew my mother would be upset, and I was too because I wanted to go back to America, but I did not really care about the baseball then." Lefty remembered the emotional toll that playing in Fort Wayne had taken on her. She recalled how poorly she had played, the struggle to understand the coaches, and her embarrassingly low statistics. It was almost a relief that she was not invited back to play in 1952. Almost.

Virtudes was so "disappointed and sad that she came up with an idea to rewrite a date on an old contract," Lefty recalls. Lefty does not know what her mother was thinking when she committed fraud to get her daughter back into the United States. It is unclear exactly what Virtudes hoped would happen by sending Lefty off to the United States without a contract, but in hindsight Lefty believes that her mother trusted that Lefty would be able to "play her way onto a team." Unbeknown to her mother, however, Lefty had no desire to play baseball that year, let alone make the effort to find a team and try out. But, Lefty continues, "She arranged for me to travel with Mickey Pérez. I think Mickey knew and went along with the plan. I don't know really." Lefty did not question her mother's dishonesty, and her confidence in Virtudes was never more fully demonstrated than when she approached immigration officials at the Havana airport in 1952 with forged papers. "She [made the changes] so perfectly that I went through immigration with no problems," Lefty says. She shakes her head and adds, "And, now, oh, Holy Cow!"

Because her stint in Battle Creek had been temporary and the old contract Virtudes "adjusted" was one for Fort Wayne, that is where Lefty went. Once back in Fort Wayne, Lefty stayed with the Finfrocks, the same family with whom she had lived in 1951. Even though the Finfrocks loved Lefty and were eager to help when she arrived in Fort Wayne that year, their home was meant to be used for current players in the league. Since she was not playing in the league, Lefty needed to find a different place to live. This fact weighed heavily on Lefty, as she was very fond of the Finfrocks, and they had become like her own family. Unsure what to do since she had no intention of reaching out to the league, Lefty spent many days wandering around trying to decide what to do next, "how to find my own way." One afternoon Lefty found herself in Waiser Park watching a women's softball game. While there, she lost a wallet with all her money and identification in it. "That is the day that changed my life forever," Lefty says. "That is the day I met Nancy Blee. While I was looking for my money, Nancy came up and asked if she could help. We spent a long time looking, and she even called the police for me. We found my wallet. Everything was just thrown all over the ground, and she took me home to meet her parents, Robert and Agnes."

Lefty was not the first immigrant that the Blees had helped transition to the United States. Nancy remembers her mother, who worked as a bookkeeper for a junkyard, helping a young Jewish man learn English. It was soon after World War II, and the family who owned the junkyard was Jewish, so they often brought young men in to work who were new to the United States. "I remember this one so well," Nancy says, "because he was from a concentration camp, and every day my mother would take time out of her day to read to him to help him learn English. It was summer, so she decided that I should take over, so every day I went to the junkyard and read to him." That experience helped create a standard for Nancy. When she saw Lefty alone and in distress, it was natural that she took her home.

The Blees gave Lefty a home and treated her like family. They looked out for her and also expected her to do chores, go to church, and participate in the family just like their own children. Mr. Blee even helped Lefty find a job at Hall's Drive-in, where she began working as a carhop. "The managers of Hall's were so nice to me," she says. "I spilled a lot of trays and the high school kids gave me a hard time, but I never once thought about quitting." She remembers that the high school boys would order a drink called chocolate seltzer, which was very difficult for her to say. "Every time I turned around to tell Mr. Hall what they wanted, they laughed at me," she remembers. "It didn't bother me, though. I just laughed too. . . . I was lucky to have the Blees to take me in; they were my family since I did not have my baseball family, but I still needed to feel like a ballplayer sometimes, so I just pretended." It was the support of the Blee family and Lefty's memory of her "sport self" that carried her through that year.

Even though Lefty did not play in 1952, baseball was probably more important to her that year than any other. Sport and the physical and emotional memory of it provided the courage Lefty needed to survive. When she was at her lowest that year in Fort Wayne, Lefty says she "relied on the memory of a time when I was good, safe, and accepted, usually playing baseball." It was not the game itself that was important to Lefty in 1952 but the memories of her time playing the game, when she felt confident and accepted. When she was working and struggling to be accepted in her new job, she pretended just like she had during those lonely days in Cuba. Remembering what it felt like to be good, to be a baseball player, made the reality of her life bearable.

During the 1952 season the AAGPBL found out that Lefty was in Fort Wayne and apparently did try to get in touch with her. Lefty recalls: "While I was in Fort Wayne, I did receive a few letters from the league asking me to play. I do not know how they found me. One letter explained that they did not have my correct address in Cuba and asked me to report. I did not answer the letters. I was just happy to be working as a carhop." There were times when baseball was too pressure-filled for Lefty and the reality of baseball was simply too stressful. She remembers that 1952 was one of those times: "Sometimes trying to understand made me feel depressed, thinking that I was not good enough. I felt very inferior to the other players; it was just a mental problem of my own, and [I] had difficulty dealing with [it] inside of me." Lefty now realizes it was not the baseball that made her feel inferior; rather she was affected by many of the same things that had made her feel so sick in school. She reflects: "It was just like how I felt in school, not good enough or smart enough; only in this case sports were wrapped up in it too, so I ran away from it all." The escape from those feelings of inferiority that she used to have as a kid in Havana was to play baseball in the streets; the need for such escape was closely connected in this case. Baseball, her refuge, was the source of the stress, so she felt lost and confused. Subconsciously, however, Lefty retreated to the playing field. "I was so sad that year when I was lost in town and with no job," she says, "but what helped me was that I pretended that I was now *la pilla* of Fort Wayne. In my mind I pretended that people here knew my reputation, so I walked taller, stronger." It was Lefty's love of sport that took over and helped her survive school when she was a child. For the adult Lefty it was the historical, physical, and emotional memory of that connection to sport that provided her with the necessary daily routine, the physical strength, and the unconscious belief that she could survive those lonely days on the streets of Fort Wayne.

By the end of 1952 Lefty felt more secure and better about herself. The year away from baseball had provided her with some distance, a chance to mature, and the time to realize just how much playing in the league meant to her. "I missed baseball very much," she says, "but mostly I missed my teammates." She was ready to return to baseball in 1953 but did not regret her decision to stay away from the league in 1952. "I am a citizen of the U.S.

because of that decision," she notes. "If I had not been wandering around Fort Wayne, I might not have met Nancy Blee and her family, and I would never have had Mr. Blee's help to become a citizen." As in previous years, Lefty had to return to Cuba at the end of the 1952 season, and it was then that her relationship with the Blees blossomed. Nancy and Lefty kept in touch as pen pals, and as difficult as the language barrier was—"I couldn't read Spanish, and she couldn't read English," Nancy recalls—they grew close. It was that close relationship with Nancy, whom she calls her sister, that set the wheels in motion for Lefty to become an American citizen.

The Blees knew that Lefty wanted to return to the United States, but of course they had no way of knowing if she would get a contract to play baseball. Rather than take that chance, Mr. Blee began the process of becoming Lefty's sponsor. For her to return to the United States without a contract to play baseball, she had to have a family willing to sponsor her. Nancy Blee recalls the process of sponsorship as being lengthy but never daunting to her parents: "The paperwork was long and difficult as I recall, and I have no idea how much it cost, but my dad and mom were happy to sponsor Isabel and were determined to make sure she could stay in the U.S. as long as she wanted. They had to promise that they would support her financially if she could not support herself and help her learn English, find a job, and a place to live." The Blees fulfilled their agreement with the United States and did much more.

Sponsorship was only the first of several steps toward Lefty's becoming a citizen, something Lefty says she did not even know she wanted until it became an option. In 1953, with the help of Mr. Blee, Lefty applied for and received residency in the United States. Getting a green card and residency gave Lefty the freedom to either play baseball or not. According to her, just knowing that fact provided her the peace of mind to make decisions about her life rather than rely on the league to make them for her. It is unclear just how Lefty smoothed things over with the league after ignoring its attempts to contact her in 1951, but she received an official contract in 1953. She was assigned to the Kalamazoo Lassies for that season, and while it was not her beloved Fort Wayne, she was happy to be playing again. It was different this time: "It was my decision to play, not anyone else's. I wanted to play."

By the time she was traded to Kalamazoo, both Lefty and the AAGPBL had changed significantly. Kalamazoo was among the teams that had experienced some of the most significant changes when the league changed management structures in 1951. One of the effects of that change was that the budget for publicity and advertising was cut from $3,300 in 1949 to $500.[19] As of October 1952 the league itself had contributed only $10.30 to publicity expenditures, leaving the rest of such expenditures to the individual teams. As a result, it was nearly impossible for teams to maintain a national presence. While some teams had more financial backing from local businessmen than others, their advertising budgets varied significantly. In 1951 Fort Wayne spent almost $3,400 on promotion and advertising alone, while the very next season, Battle Creek was capable of spending only approximately $250 to maintain interest in its team.[20] Meyerhoff and Wrigley both believed that the more spent on advertising, the more money one could make; by the early 1950s the individual team owners did not adhere to that philosophy. The profit-loss report for the South Bend Blue Sox during the 1953 season illustrates this fact. Roughly $1,600 was spent specifically on publicity and advertising, but operating costs and low attendance resulted in a loss of almost $8,000 during that year.[21]

As a result of the league's shift from centralized to individual-owner management and the loss of money and fans, teams moved to new towns and cities looking for new fan bases. The Muskegon Lassies began their 1950 season in Muskegon, but by midseason they had moved to Kalamazoo. Midway through the season (and still in their Muskegon uniforms), the Kalamazoo Lassies played their first game at Lindstrom Field in their new hometown. An enthusiastic crowd of about fourteen hundred attended the game. From 1950 to 1953, when Lefty was receiving contracts to play for the Lassies, the team struggled to attain a winning season. The Lassies ended 1951 with a record of thirty-three wins, seventy-five losses, and two ties. In 1952 the team finished fifth of six teams with a 49-60 record, and in 1953 it finished third and reached the playoffs for the first time.

It was in this struggling atmosphere in the spring of 1953 that Lefty had to start over yet again. It was as hard for Lefty to leave Fort Wayne and the Blees as it had been for her to leave Havana. "I was sad to leave them," she says. "I was settled there, had a home and a caring family. I had a job, but . . . I wanted to play ball that year, so I had to go."[22] As hard as it was for her to move from Fort Wayne to Kalamazoo, however, she was comforted by the fact that the Blees did not stop loving Nancy when she went away to college, making it seem more likely that she would continue to be loved by them as well, even in Kalamazoo. "Nancy went to college, and I went to Kalamazoo; that's all. I saw how they still loved her and just knew they would treat me like that too." Indeed they did.

Kalamazoo was similar in size to Fort Wayne and just over an hour's drive away. Lefty remembers: "I knew it wasn't too far. I couldn't go there much, but I knew it was close. That [knowledge] helped me, I think." She enjoyed her time in Kalamazoo, even though it was hard getting used to a new team, new coaches, and a new city. It was a big help that Mitch Skupien was the manager of the Lassies that year. Before taking the reins of the Lassies, Skupien had managed the Rayson Sporting Goods, a Chicago baseball team, and had served as a scout for the AAGPBL. In his first management job for the AAGPBL, in 1951 with the Grand Rapids Chicks, Skupien led the team to the first-half title with a 40-13 record. The team earned a spot in the playoffs but lost the first round to the Rockford Peaches.[23]

Hoping he would be able to revive the struggling Kalamazoo Lassies, the league sent Skupien to Kalamazoo in 1952. With Skupien as manager the Lassies did improve but ended the season next to last. In 1953, the year Lefty played for them, the Lassies finished third, with a 53-50 record, and advanced to the playoffs. Despite the team's relative success, however, Lefty remembers little about her playing time and more about her manager's kindness and the relationships she was able to develop. She liked Skupien: "He was nice to me, helped me to understand things better. Sometimes other people would get impatient with me because I did not understand the language, but he did not, and it meant a lot to me. I learned the game better but also did not have that inferiority complex I had before." Skupien's demeanor helped make Lefty's transition to the Lassies a bit smoother, but she still had to find her way off the field too.

Lefty made lifelong friends while in Kalamazoo. During that season she lived with Terry Rukavina and Ange Armato. Rukavina had already been playing in the league for three years by the time Lefty met her. She had joined the Chicago Colleens and Springfield Sallies touring teams in 1950 and had hit .271, with 4 home runs and 71 RBIs in 77 games. She then filled in at many different infield and outfield positions with the Kalamazoo Lassies in 1951 and 1953, hitting .163, with 1 homer and 23 RBIs in 147 games. Armato appeared in only a few games for the Lassies during the 1953 season. Lefty remembers both women fondly. She had an apartment on the second floor of their old house; she loved living there and "adjusted well with them. . . . We became good friends, and through them I met other friends." The year spent in Kalamazoo was freer, more fun than the previous years had been. Lefty attributes that to her own maturity and to her finally learning to speak English. At least she could understand more of what the coaches wanted and could make closer friends on the team. "When I got better at understanding, I learned that people liked me," she says. "The language and difference in culture were hard, but finally I made friends."

Lefty's time on the field as a Kalamazoo Lassie was also more satisfying because she did not have to pitch all the time. Pitchers are the center of attention and carry the weight of the game, making it a very stressful position to play. It is they who are credited with either winning or losing a game. The pressure of that position added to Lefty's anxiety and feelings of inadequacy. As a pitcher, Lefty's lack of confidence often got in the way of good play on the field. In Kalamazoo, however, she was more relaxed in part because she did not have the pressure of pitching. She did not pitch at all that year but played as a utility outfielder and achieved her second highest batting average. In 53 games she had 123 at bats, 24 hits, and 12 RBIs for a .195 average. While a .195 batting average is certainly not going to win any batting titles, for Lefty it was an improvement and a sign that she "could play this game."

Because Lefty had a green card and residency, she did not have to return to Cuba after the 1953 season, a fact that both thrilled and terrified her. She wanted to remain in the United States, and it wasn't until many years later that she realized how hard that was for her mother. "I did not want to go back home," she says. "I just wanted to stay here and be free. I did not even think about my mother missing me. She did though. I know now she did." After the season ended, Lefty returned to the Blee home for the off-season, but after having had more independence, she found it harder to live under their house rules. She explains: "When I moved back to Fort Wayne, some of my friends from Kalamazoo came to visit me. They were men and I think they looked odd, so Mr. and Mrs. Blee did not like them to visit. They protected me as they did Nancy." When pushed to explain who these men were and what she means by "odd," she just shrugs. "I don't know. They were men, and the Blees did not like them." It was both comforting and frustrating that the Blees treated Lefty like one of their own children, she says: "The Blees treated me like a daughter and that made me happy, but I did not want restrictions."

On more than one occasion Lefty's "stubborn streak" ran headlong into that of Mr. Blee. "I did not have a car, and Mr. Blee was always worried about my walking to work and home alone," she says. "So I tried to buy a car once, but Mr. Blee put a stop to it." During the 1953 season Lefty saved $700 and wanted to use the money to buy a used car: "I don't remember what kind it was, only that it was black with two doors. The person selling the car brought it to Mr. Blee's house for him to see. [Mr. Blee] said, 'You are not buying this car. How are you going to buy gas?' I did not think about that, only the price for the car." At the time Lefty did not have a driver's license or insurance and most certainly did not know how to drive. The Blees were a strong Catholic family, and Lefty remembers that Mrs. Blee insisted that she go to church and donate to the church every week. When Mr. Blee gave her a little box of envelopes to use for her weekly donations, Lefty asked him, "Why do I have to do this? If I have money to put in these little envelopes, then I could have money for gas." Lefty remembers Mr. Blee's facial expression but not his words. "He looked kind of red," she says with a laugh.

Lefty is also aware that she was very lucky to have the Blees in her life. "What would have happened to me if not for the Blees?" she asks. "I would have given my money to that man and tried to drive off in that car." This story illustrates how Lefty lived in those early years, with an abundance of courage and naiveté. Trusting things would work out, Lefty dove into life head first, and, as she readily admits, sometimes it worked but often it did not. Yet, she says, "It was always an adventure." Mr. Blee would no doubt agree. After Lefty's attempt to buy a car, he taught her to drive. According to Nancy, "Dad took her off to a big parking lot, showed her about the clutch and the gears and then let her behind the wheel. 'She has only two speeds,' he said later, 'stopped and fast.'" When hearing Nancy tell that story, Lefty laughs, shakes her head, and says, "That is still true."

As Lefty got more comfortable with the Blees and with living in Fort Wayne, she began to make more friends and to carve out a life separate from them. While working at Hall's Drive-in, Lefty remarks, "I do not remember that any of my Daisies teammates visited me. Just Bill Arlington [the manager]. It was in 1954 (fifty-seven years ago); I was twenty-one years old. Lefty found a friend and a kindred spirit in Dona Schaefer, a friend of the Finfrocks. Dona, working-class and struggling to make ends meet, held various jobs and lived with her grandmother when she and Lefty met. Lefty could relate to Dona's struggles, and because Dona was an active member of the softball community in Fort Wayne, they could also bond over sports. The two became close friends very quickly, so when Dona decided to move from her grandmother's house to the family farm, she asked Lefty to move with her.

The timing was fortunate as it was around that time that Mrs. Blee asked Lefty to move out on her own. Lefty explains: "Mrs. Blee told me I had to move on. She was very active and going out a lot. She told me that staying alone with Mr. Blee when she was not there might make neighbors talk with malice since I was so young. Dona told me that I could live out in the farm with her three sisters, two brothers, and her mom and dad. She moved back home when I accepted her offer. Dona had a car, so we took off." Even though she insisted that Lefty move out of their house, Mrs. Blee remained protective of her. "When I met Dona," Lefty remembers, "Mrs. Blee made a brief remark that she did not like her. I think it was because she was poor and did not have a good job." It is hard to know if Dona's working-class background was an issue for Agnes Blee or if it was something else about Lefty's friend. Either way it is clear that Lefty's safety and well-being were of concern to her. Still Lefty packed her few belongings into Dona's old car, and the two of them set off for Dona's family farm. The experience of moving to the farm, away from the Blees and other friends, was challenging for Lefty. She felt isolated and always in the way of Dona's family. Yet the experience was important for Lefty's growth and maturity, and when it was time to report for the 1954 season, she was a more confident individual and ready to play for yet another team, the Grand Rapids Chicks.

As the AAGPBL struggled to maintain equity among the teams and to draw fans, many players were moved from team to team. Lefty was no exception. In 1953 the Chicks had been the playoff champions, so Lefty was excited to join the team despite her nervousness about another new team. Lefty enjoyed her time in Grand Rapids: "I liked Grand Rapids. People there were nice, and it was a good place for me. I hardly ever had to pretend I was okay; I mostly was." She did not have time to settle in there as her stint with Grand Rapids was short-lived. Lefty was traded back to Fort Wayne in midseason. "Even though I liked Grand Rapids, I was glad to go back home to Fort Wayne," she says. "It was home."

Lefty's return to Fort Wayne ended up being bittersweet. In many ways Lefty's 1954 season was one of her most difficult. Beginning the season in Grand Rapids and trying to settle in a new place was not as hard for Lefty as it might have been some years before, but Lefty's last year in the league was both emotionally and physically painful. She had been back in Fort Wayne only a short time when she was injured in a game. "I was running to first base," she remembers. "I rounded the bag, and when returning to the base, I twisted my knee." Lefty remembers being helped from the field and then transported to the hospital. It was a scary time. The language barrier often made her unsure of what was happening during treatment. "While in the hospital, I had a lot of visitors at first," she says. "Even Max Carey [who had been her manager in 1950 and 1951] and Bill Arlington [her current manager] came to see me at the hospital; he asked me questions that I just cannot remember. Also Mickey Pérez, my best friend of all the Cuban players and my roommate when we played in the touring team, came to see me. Then, because I was in there so long, people stopped coming." Lefty's treatment required that she remain in the hospital in traction for a month to repair what she believes were torn ligaments. She is unsure how long it took her to fully heal, but the memory of the physical and emotional pain is vivid. "I don't think I ever felt that alone," she says. "I didn't have my friends on the team around me and didn't understand what was happening. I was scared and lonely. Holy cow!" Since most of her relationships were tied to the league, the lengthy hospital stay time away from baseball and an uncertain future made that time one of her worst.

Lefty had no idea the AAGPBL was nearing its end. By 1954 changes to the league's administration and a growing interest in Major League baseball on television had caught up with the league. As money tightened, team owners started looking for places to cut back. Rookie training teams, such as the Colleens and Sallies, were among the first to go. The immediate result was a shallow recruiting pool and a serious lack of talent coming into the league. In 1952 the Kenosha and Peoria teams were disbanded, leaving only six teams in the league. In 1953 the Battle Creek team relocated to Muskegon, and by the end of the season it too had folded. When the league ended in 1954, only five teams remained: Fort Wayne, South Bend, Grand Rapids, Kalamazoo, and Rockford.[24]

As the future of the league came into question in the final years, area newspapers proclaimed its uncertainty. As early as September 1953 newspapers in league cities began printing articles on its possible failings.[25] In November 1953 the *Chicago Sunday Tribune* went so far as to publish a claim that the Rockford Peaches had given up hope of playing the 1954 season. In the early months of 1954 rumors still appeared in the newspapers regarding the league's continuation.[26] In mid-February, Joe Doyle, a writer for the *South Bend Tribune*, reported that the league was unlikely to play in 1954.[27] Even though the league's board voted to suspend play on January 25, another board meeting on February 22 addressed the public's response to the loss of women's baseball and the need to consider new ways of continuing the league.[28] The articles that seemed skeptical of the league's continuation may have generated enough concern to continue the league in its final year, as league directors overturned their vote of suspension and authorized play in the 1954 season.[29]

In April 1954 *Daisy Fan News*, the newsletter for the Fort Wayne Daisies Fan Club, addressed the problems facing the Daisies and their fellow league teams.[30] Aware of the league's near suspension for the 1954 season, the newsletter appealed to the fans and their potential to save the league. It emphasized that the "pressure and desire of the many fans" had made the 1954 season possible, and it urged loyal fans to do even more if they hoped for another season.[31] The primary reason that the league's board of directors had considered suspending play in 1954 was the loss of over $80,000 in the 1953 season.[32] To show appreciation for the game and the league's decision to continue playing, the Daisies' fan club urged its members to purchase tickets and to help the league emphasize that the game the teams played was baseball, not softball.[33]

Many members of the AAGPBL began the 1954 season understanding the pressure of needing to make up the money lost in 1953. For the league to continue—a proposition that they knew was uncertain—the players knew they had to be successful. Despite the fans' push to keep the league going, teams were unable to make up for the league's financial losses after the 1953 season, and the board of directors pulled the plug on the league after the 1954 season. The board's reluctance to end the league was evident, however, because it created plans and contingencies for a 1955 season in case the fans were able to spark enough interest to keep the league afloat.[34] The plans indicated interest from Grand Rapids and South Bend, and a newspaper article from early 1955 reported that Fort Wayne and Kalamazoo were also ready to play another season.[35] It was in late January 1955, however, that the *Kalamazoo Gazette* reported that the league would disband at the end of that month.[36] The 1954 season was the league's last. Many players had been aware of the league's struggles, so the end came as no surprise. Lefty did not have the same insight about the league as some of the other players; therefore, she was unprepared for the league's demise.

In fact Lefty would not return to professional baseball after her devastating knee injury. She remembers the feeling of loss as she says, "The league just ended. I got hurt, and it was just gone." It is hard to imagine why, but for some reason the team seemed to abandon Lefty at the end of the 1954 season. Each year there was an all-star game to end the season. That game in 1954 did not include Lefty, and she is not pictured in any of the end-of-season photographs. "They did not give me my uniform back since I could not get back in the game or be seated in the bench as an injured player," she remembers. She was not going to attend the game at all, but a local Mexican family who had befriended Lefty thought it was wrong that she was not allowed to participate in the game, even as a benchwarmer. So they took her to the game. She sat in the stands with them and watched the game. That was her last contact with the league.

The memories of that time are difficult ones for Lefty. "I didn't know what to do," she says. "I tried remembering my sport self, but it didn't work. It was like I knew that was gone, and it just didn't help me anymore." During other difficult times for Lefty she was able to rely on the place and the feeling of being good—a "real *pilla*"—but once that part of her was damaged, she was unable to rely on it for strength and comfort. Unfortunately this time in the summer of 1954 was not the last time Lefty was unable to call up those positive memories of her "sport self." From 1954 onward Lefty's life became more and more difficult, and she faced challenges that she could have never imagined when she first came to America.

1. Prudencio Eusébio Álvarez de León Valdés and María Virtudes Cerdán Fernández. Lefty believes this was taken shortly after their wedding.

2. Prudencio Eusébio Álvarez de León Valdés.

3. Prudencio Eusébio Álvarez de León Valdés. Lefty is not sure of her father's age here, but she says, "It shows how much of a dandy my father was."

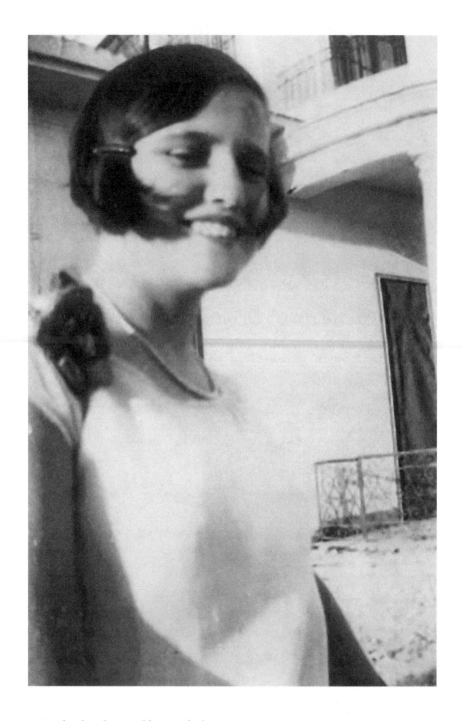

4. María Virtudes Cerdán Fernández.

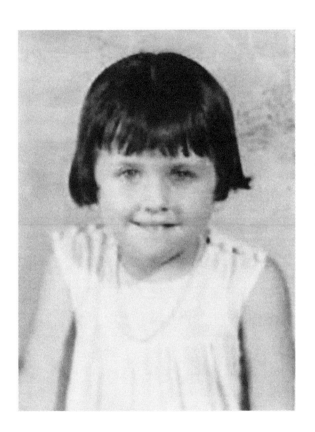

5. Isabel "Lefty" Alvarez. Age unknown.

6. Lefty's brother, Antonio, and Lefty. Ages unknown.

7. Lefty, Antonio, and their mother. Date unknown.

8. Lefty's mother was determined to put Lefty in every "respectable" sport possible. Fencing fit that bill, and Lefty was quite good.

9. Lefty in her volleyball uniform. Volleyball was one of Lefty's favorite sports.

10. Lefty showing her athletic ability.

11. Lefty in her Estrellas Cubanas uniform.

12. Lefty's AAGPBL baseball card. Courtesy of Larry Fritsch Cards, Stevens Point, Wisconsin, www.FritschCards.com.

13. Lefty, probably in 1949 or 1950.

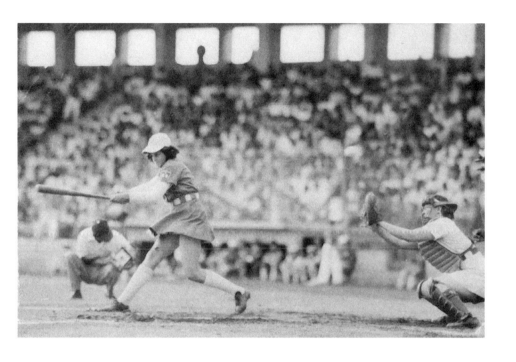

14. Lefty batting, probably in 1949 or 1950.

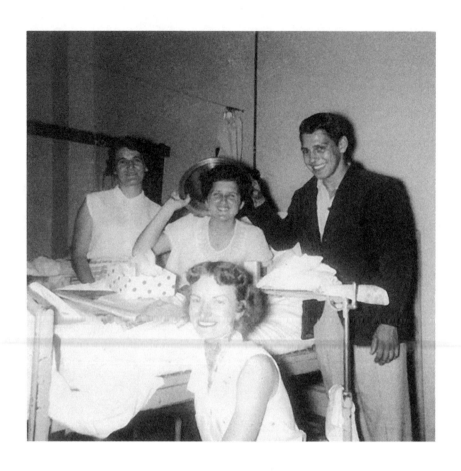

15. Lefty surrounded by friends in the hospital after her career-ending injury, 1954.

16. Former AAGPBL players registering for the Run, Jane, Run event, 1980.

17. Lefty (left) and Doris "Cookie" Cook at the Run, Jane, Run event in 1981.

18. Lefty having fun at the Run, Jane, Run event in 1981.

19. Terry Donahue, Jane Moffet, and Lefty (right) at the Houston reunion banquet, 2006. Photo by author.

20. Lefty (left) and Jane Moffet. Photo by author.

21. Lefty surrounded by admirers at the 2016 dedication of the International Women's Baseball Center. Photo by author.

22. Kat Williams, Donna Cohen, and Lefty (right) at the 2016 dedication of the International Women's Baseball Center. Photo by author.

23. Kat Williams and Lefty on a reunion cruise, 2008. Photo by author.

CHAPTER FIVE

Life after the League

Holy Cow! Did I have some life after the League!

LEFTY ALVAREZ

When the AAGPBL ended in 1954, many of its players went to college, got married, or returned to their hometowns. Lefty Alvarez did none of those things. Because her education had ended at the sixth grade, college was not an option, although she would try to continue her education. Friendships were important to her, but Lefty had an inclination to keep friends at arm's length, and she never married. She did not want to return to Cuba to live under Virtudes Álvarez's watchful eye. So Lefty decided to stay in Fort Wayne, which she considered "home." She says, "[It was] a place where I had friends, a life outside my family in Cuba." As discussed in chapter 4, Lefty already had worked as a carhop at Hall's Drive-in. As it turned out, Lefty needed the comfort of a familiar place and the support of friends just to survive the years after baseball. The league ended just as Lefty was coming of age, becoming a young woman. This period in one's life can be a difficult time for anyone, but for Lefty it overlapped with the loss of her profession and with her trying to find her footing in a new country. This combination shaped the next decade of Lefty's life.

Lefty was twenty-one years old in 1954. She was a beautiful young woman, with long dark hair and eyes that, as Nancy Blee remembers, "seemed to sparkle with mischief." She had a job and supported herself. She got attention from a lot of men, and a number of friends, including the Blees, continued to look after her. It was almost as if Lefty collected people. From the male friends who visited her from South Bend (and who so distressed the Blees) to the scores of people, mostly unnamed, who helped her at different times in her life, Lefty was often surrounded by people. In photographs of Lefty in the hospital after her knee injury, she is surrounded by people, male and female. Nurses are gathered around the hospital bed, smiling down at her. Although Lefty was unable to identify any of these individuals, they are evidence that people seemed always to be there for her when she needed help. On the surface her new life in America looked just like the one Virtudes had dreamed she would have, but inwardly Lefty struggled. She remembers that time as very lonely.

Losing the league, the structure and built-in sense of family and community it provided, was hard for Lefty. Her English was still spotty, an obstacle that continued to make it difficult for her to communicate. Despite Lefty's tumultuous relationship with her family, estrangement from it was hard. The only communication with her parents came through letters written by her mother. Lefty did not remember any letters to her from Prudencio or her brother Tony. She was clear that she did not miss being in Cuba with them: "No matter what, I did not want to go back to that mess. I was better off without them." She may not have wanted to return to Cuba or even maintain a solid relationship with her family, but that loss contributed to her feelings of loneliness.

Lefty had also lost the other Cuban players who had been her friends and part of a support system. By the league's end all three Cuban players who had come to the United States in the same year as Lefty—Ysora Castillo, Mirtha Marrero, and Migdalia Pérez—had gone their separate ways. Castillo left the league in 1951 and Marrero in 1953. Pérez, Lefty's travel partner and close friend during her early days in the AAGPBL, was involved with the league until 1954. She had been especially important to Lefty, and, as Lefty says, "helped me understand the ways of the U.S." While Pérez played in Rockford that last year, reducing the contact between them, "knowing Mickey was in the league helped me. I always felt alone [as a Cuban], but I knew she was in the league too." After the league ended, Mickey also disappeared from Lefty's life. Lefty had no contact with any of the Cuban players after the league ended, and years later she remembers feeling she was "the only Cuban in the country." She laughs at that memory, knowing it wasn't really true, "but it felt like it. I was alone. Even though I did not see them very much, we were part of the All-Americans together, and that helped me." Lefty's feeling of being the "only Cuban" made it even harder for her to adjust to a new life once her baseball career ended.

Lefty's sense of loneliness stemmed from her difficulties connecting with people on a deeper level. When Lefty felt bad about herself, had conflicts with others, or was simply having a hard time at work, her default position was always to retreat. She would withdraw into herself and keep others at a distance. The years after the league's end were no different. It is possible that Lefty's early life in Cuba, where her mother taught her to be mistrustful of people, affected her ability to be close to people as an adult.

In a joint interview with former AAGPBL player and friend, Maybelle Blair, Lefty says that she never told anyone she loved them. Blair asks her why. "I don't know," Lefty responds. "Well, did you love people? You love me, don't you?" Blair urges. Lefty begins to cry. "Yes, I love you, Maybelle. I have loved people, but they never knew. I just never could tell them." Blair makes Lefty promise she would always tell her friends she loved them when she talked on the phone or saw them in person. From that day on Lefty did just that. This exchange helps to explain why, despite numerous friends who cared for her, Lefty's feelings of isolation deepened.

Finding better employment was Lefty's focus in this period. Virtudes's insistence that Lefty "make something of herself" drove her desire for a better job, but a lack of education made that difficult for her. "Everywhere I applied asked about high school," she remembers. "You had to circle the number of the highest grade completed, and I knew that I could only circle "6," so that held me back." Lefty decided to go to night school and try to earn a GED. Not only did Lefty know that having only a sixth-grade education was a detriment to finding a well-paid job, but also, as she recalls much later, she was embarrassed by being so uneducated. She had friends who encouraged her ambition and drove her to classes at a local school, but despite their support Lefty could not finish the high school equivalency course. Time had not erased her learning disability and the struggles she had had in school. Lefty relied on old coping tools this time too: "It was just like when I was a kid and my mother let me stay home; I had that inferiority complex and just could not learn." But instead of staying home, Lefty hid in the bathroom every night rather than going to class. One day her friends came early to pick her up and saw her feet under a bathroom stall. She had to tell them the truth—that she just could not face going to school. Lefty was embarrassed that she had mislead her friends, but the fear of attending class was just too overwhelming.

At that point Lefty accepted that a formal education was not in her future and decided that she would have to survive without one. This decision was understandable, and she felt relieved at the time. But later Lefty regretted that she gave up on education and in many ways blamed her mother for that decision: "My mother always said it was okay; I could be something without [education]. I believed her because it was easier [to do so]. That's why I gave up on classes. She said it was okay, and I believed it." The memory of her mother's leniency about school made Lefty angry. "I know it is not fair really," she says, "but I am mad about that with her. She should have made me go [to school], but she did not care. She did not have much schooling, and I was happy to be home, so she did not make me go. Why did she do that?" Lefty's assumption that Virtudes did not care about her education seems accurate on the surface. She did not force Lefty to attend school or even seem upset by her lack of education. But it is important to place Virtudes within the context of her own upbringing in Cuba. Girls were not expected to be formally educated, and Virtudes herself had little education. Even though she sought a better life for Lefty, it makes sense that education would not have been the path Virtudes chose to accomplish that goal. Regardless of the reasons, Lefty did not have an educational foundation to succeed in the classroom; eventually she accepted the fact and set out to find other routes to a good and fulfilling life.

Lefty found work for better pay at the Fort Wayne Tailoring Company, which, despite its name, was a manufacturing company producing ready-made clothing. Lefty felt good about the job and the increased income. But when pushed to talk about the job and what she did there, she confesses to having little memory of it: "I was running around with my friends back then. My friend Dona Schaefer and I spent a lot of time together. She had a car and would drop me off at work and pick me up after work."[1] The job itself was not nearly as important as what it allowed her to do. Life was getting better for Lefty.

But just as Lefty was settling into her life, it was upended again. Dona Schaefer had been working for the Indiana Michigan Electric Company, but around 1955 she was offered a better job that required moving to South Bend for four or five months of training. Dona insisted that Lefty go with her. In fact she told Lefty that she would not take the new job if Lefty did not go to South Bend with her. "I believe that she meant it," Lefty says, "so I said I'd go. I had some of my own money—the $700 I was going to use to buy a car—so she said we could use that money, and I would not have to find a job as soon as we got there."

To make the situation more awkward, Lefty found out later that three other girls who were also part of the training program would be joining them in a small South Bend apartment. All five women stayed in one room. Lefty was uncomfortable sharing a bed and a room with women she did not know very well. "I do not remember how many beds there were, but I was not comfortable, and I had to find a job," she recalls, "and I had no idea what to do." Lefty found herself in yet another new place—this time against her better judgment.

Since the training program was for only a few months, Lefty knew that her time in South Bend was limited, making it hard to find a job. But she also knew that finding employment was both financially and emotionally important. It was hard for Lefty to simply do nothing as "they [the other girls] were all going off to their school and me just there in that room. It was a bad time." Lefty finally found a job at Wilson Brothers, a clothing manufacturer: "We made shirts. I found where it was and took the bus. After all these years, I ask myself, 'How did you do it?' I guess it was my stubbornness." The time at work saved her during those months in South Bend, keeping her busy and out of the small apartment. But the memory of that time is still quite painful.

Lefty remarks: "After I left the Blees' house [to move in with the Schaefer family], my life started to be a nightmare. I did not want to be tied down to one person—too much pressure—but I did not have any way out with Dona. I do not like to hurt people who try in their own way to help me, and I know that Dona tried to help me sometimes." This kind of conflict was not new for her. Lefty was naïve and often unable to communicate what she needed in those early years. She always wanted to please people—a trait instilled in her by Virtudes—and admits that that part of her personality often got her in trouble: "I cannot say no to people. That is trouble sometimes, but I do not want to disappoint them." This became a recurring theme in Lefty's and Dona's relationship. The result was that Dona, who understood Lefty's weaknesses and knew how to convince Lefty to do what she wanted, often seemed to control her. Lefty did not see a way out of the situation, so she tended to give in and simply withdraw inside herself. Lefty's relationship with Dona continued to be complicated, although it also sustained her.

When Dona's training was over, she and Lefty returned to the Shafer family farm outside Fort Wayne. Lefty was not able to return to her work for Fort Wayne Tailoring and, unsure of her next step, began suffering from anxiety. Finally, after being pushed by Dona's mother, she got a job waitressing at a local bar and restaurant, the Nine Mile. In this period Lefty found herself once again playing ball and being recognized as a ballplayer, although this time she was playing softball.

Softball was enormously popular in the Midwest in the 1950s and 1960s. The Amateur Softball Association was established in 1934, and by the mid-1940s there were roughly six hundred thousand teams across the United States.[2] Many of these teams played in the Midwest. There were separate men's and women's teams sponsored by parks, churches, businesses, and community organizations such as the American Turners, a national organization founded in Cincinnati, Ohio, in 1848 by German immigrants. The organization's goal is to encourage and facilitate physical activity in the lives of individuals. Its motto, "A Sound Mind in a Sound Body," goes a long way toward explaining its purpose. Initially Turners was associated with gymnastics. (The name "Turners" comes from the German word for "gymnast.") But soon the various facilities began sponsoring other sports, and by the mid-twentieth century they were best known for their recreational softball leagues. It was at the Fort Wayne Turners that Lefty played softball.

Turners was, until only a few years ago, an important part of Lefty's community. Turners and the softball community in Fort Wayne gave her a new place to belong and a place that was focused on sports. Fort Wayne Turners sponsored men's and women's softball leagues, and by the 1960s the organization relied on those leagues for survival. The 1960s would mark a downturn in Turners membership. High school and college athletes were restricted from taking part in sports programs not affiliated with their schools. In the 1960s a lot of people moved from the city centers, where many Turners societies were located, to the suburbs. This resulted in members leaving the group. The one constant, however, was softball. Both men's and women's leagues continued to be popular throughout the 1960s.

During the late 1950s and early 1960s Lefty played on a Turners team coached by Dona Schaefer. For Lefty being part of a team again was important. She loved the game. Even though it wasn't baseball, it was a sport, and she had missed playing one. As a team member, she had fun, was able to compete, and once again felt the happiness associated with being around teammates. But while playing softball at Turners was a godsend, it was also a curse. While Lefty was "hanging out with that softball crowd," she was introduced to things "[I] never did while playing [professional] ball," particularly drinking and smoking. At first drinking was a relief for Lefty: "Everybody drank beer, so I did too," she recalls. "It made me happy, and I did not worry. I worry so much most of the time, it was nice not to, so I drank." Alcohol had not been part of Lefty's life before. During her childhood in Cuba alcohol was rarely used by members of her family. Certainly her mother never would have permitted Lefty to drink. Because her own father had been a very violent alcoholic, Virtudes was adamant that neither Tony nor Lefty drink alcohol. Later, while in the AAGPBL, Lefty did not drink because the league had very strict rules against it. As an adult playing softball, however, Lefty began drinking. As she understands now, "It was just a way to forget." Alcohol most certainly helped ease the loneliness and pain, but it also became a serious problem for Lefty.

The complexities of Lefty and Dona's relationship may have increased the anxiety Lefty was experiencing. Dona liked the idea that she had a former professional baseball player on her team. She encouraged, even insisted, that Lefty continue playing softball, even when a doctor told Lefty to stop playing or risk further damage to her knees. While Dona no doubt has a different memory of the time, Lefty remembers that Dona convinced her that Dona's happiness and even her well-being were tied to Lefty's presence on the field. "I am angry even now because I told her I couldn't, that I shouldn't play, but she liked the celebrity that came from having a former All-American on her team," she laments. "It made her more important, and she did not care what it did to me." It was Lefty's decision to play, but she was very easy to manipulate, and it was that characteristic and the fact that Dona took advantage of it that hurts Lefty today. "I know I am responsible for myself," she says, "but she knew I would do what she wanted, even if it hurt me. She knew." Eventually Lefty had surgery on both knees, but as she now understands, her anger at Dona was not about her ailing knees but something else altogether: "I am upset with her because she used me, and mostly I am mad at myself for letting her."

Lefty endured, and despite it all she was able to have a life that made her proud. While she wasn't always successful at it, Lefty did learn to stick up for herself. As noted, with the help of friends who encouraged her, Lefty tried to get a high school education; although she failed to do so, she learned from that experience. "I had good friends who helped me," she says. "I found that out for sure." On some level, knowing she had those friends, even if she kept them at arm's length, made other difficulties bearable. Lefty had found gainful employment at Fort Wayne Tailoring, and even though she had left that job for South Bend, that experience helped her too. Lefty liked the job at the tailoring company, and "It made me know I could get a good job. It helped knowing that when I had to keep trying for [another] job." Life was hard for Lefty in the 1950s, but it was a life she had created. Despite what she sees as controlling behavior by some friends and some very bad decisions on her part, Lefty realizes she also made some good decisions. Maintaining a relationship with the Blees was one. The Blees provided a constant in her life, and they provided a level of security she desperately needed.

As much as they could while she lived elsewhere, the Blees continued to watch out for Lefty. They offered advice on jobs, automobile purchases, and even Lefty's friends. Lefty admits she rarely took their advice. Much like a young adult reacts to parents, Lefty wanted the Blees' advice but also felt pride in being able to reject it. She remembers with a laugh that she often "just decided to do things my way. I do not think Mr. Blee liked it, but I was stubborn." While the Blees helped to create a sense of security for Lefty, one suggestion by Mr. Blee thrust her and Nancy Blee into turmoil.

In 1957 Mr. Blee became determined that Lefty and Nancy should visit Lefty's family in Cuba. Nancy Blee said she was not sure if her father simply thought it was time for Lefty to reconnect with her family or if he had knowledge of the unrest in Cuba at the time and wanted Lefty to make a trip home for what might be a last visit with her parents. In either case, he was equally determined that Lefty should not go by herself. This time Lefty took his advice. That March the Blees drove Lefty and Nancy to Miami, where the young women boarded a plane for Cuba. It seems that none of them had any real idea of what would face them there.

Cuba, as it turned out, was in the middle of a crisis. The Cuban Revolution had begun on July 26, 1953, when Fidel Castro led a group of 160 rebels in an attack against the Moncada military base in Santiago de Cuba as part of a campaign to overthrow Cuban dictator Fulgencio Batista y Zaldívar.[3] The group was small and not well armed, so nearly all in it were killed. Castro was arrested but later given amnesty. Che Guevara joined Castro's movement, and the two, along with Raúl Castro, led the revolution from Cuba's Sierra Maestra mountains. From there they waged a guerrilla campaign against the Batista government by attacking oil facilities, government buildings, and radio stations. These assaults lead to a crackdown on any known or suspected rebels.

The simmering conflict erupted into all-out civil war on March 13, 1957. In broad daylight and in the middle of Havana traffic a group of revolutionaries—a group from the Student Revolutionary Directorate (RD; Directorio Revolucionario Estudiantil) attacked the presidential palace in a failed attempt to assassinate President Batista. Simultaneously a second group of RD rebels was involved in a shootout with Batista's forces as they attempted to seize the Havana radio station. RD leader, student José Antonio Echeverría, died in the fight. After this encounter Batista's forces were heavily armed and on high alert. A few days later Lefty Alvarez and Nancy Blee arrived at the Havana airport.

Naturally Nancy expected that Lefty had contacted her parents about the upcoming visit, and "[I] thought the family would meet us at the airport when we landed, but no family. So we got a taxi to Isabel's house . . . (she is still 'Isabel' to me). The cab had barely slowed down when she jumped out of the car and ran into the house, yelling, 'Mama, I am here, I am here.'" In fact Lefty had neglected to tell her parents that they were coming. As she later recalled, "I nearly gave my mother a heart attack." When asked about why she did not tell her parents, Lefty simply shrugs and says, "I just wanted to surprise them, I guess." There was almost certainly more to it than that. As Nancy recalls, throughout the visit Lefty seemed to enjoy antagonizing her mother. She remembers that "it was as if Isabel was waiting on Virtudes to tell her what to do all the time just so she could ignore her." When pressed about what was going on, Lefty simply changes the subject. With a laugh and a shake of the head she says, "My father was not happy because I scared my mother but also because there was trouble in Cuba."

There was reason for Prudencio to be upset. The family had been further divided by the political crisis. Prudencio was a staunch follower of Batista and his government. Tony, Lefty's brother, was a supporter of the revolution. The two men could barely speak to one another without fighting, yet they continued to live in the same house. To add to the tension, the family was still struggling financially. And now Virtudes's one shining spot, Lefty, had nearly frightened her mother to death.

Nancy remembers that once Virtudes regained her composure, it seemed that she was happy to see Lefty and Nancy. Nancy did not speak Spanish and had no idea what they were saying much of the time. So later that day, after what seemed like a serious conversation between Lefty and her mother, when Lefty suggested that they head downtown to sightsee, Nancy eagerly went along. Nancy and Lefty boarded a city bus and headed to town. "She waltzed me right into the heart of the revolution," Nancy recalls with a laugh. "I was terrified at the sight of soldiers with machine guns, but she seemed unfazed. In fact she asked to have her picture taken with two of them. I thought we were going to be shot. They kept saying, 'Alto, alto, [stop, stop].' Isabel acted like she didn't speak Spanish, and of course she was very attractive, so they finally gave in, and I took her picture with these armed soldiers." Lefty was either naïve, stubborn, attention-seeking, or quite possibly defiant when she knowingly led them into that danger. But she too laughs at the memory, dismissing it with, "Well, I just didn't get upset about such things, I guess."

Nancy, however, was upset, and many years later remembers her fear: "The steps of the palace had machine gunners seated behind their big guns on tripods. There was all sorts of noise going off, and we decided to take some cover in the elevator of an office building. We went to the bottom floor and flipped a switch to keep anyone else from pulling the elevator back up. After the noise upstairs near the palace quieted down, we went back up. I said we needed to go home, and she agreed." As Lefty and Nancy made their way out of the center of Havana and to a bus stop, they came across a woman who had a litter of puppies. Incomprehensibly Lefty told Nancy she wanted a puppy, and she took one. A few blocks later, when they arrived at the bus stop, they were told they could not get on the bus with the puppy, so they had to walk all the way back to Lefty's home. From the city center to Lefty's house was just under three miles, but both say it felt longer. The two young women finally showed up at Lefty's parents' house exhausted, scared, and carrying a puppy. When he realized they had been in the city center, Prudencio was furious, but the fact that they had walked all the way home with a puppy simply rendered him speechless. In a move that must have been familiar to Lefty from her childhood, "He shook his head and walked away."

After that incident Prudencio kept a close eye on the girls, and after only a few days he insisted that they should return to the United States immediately. Early the next morning they were at the airport. Nancy recalls that they were separated at the airport since she was North American and Lefty was Cuban. "I was interrogated by some people in Spanish. They eventually gave up because I kept saying I wanted to go to the U.S. Embassy. I had probably heard that in a movie. Obviously we got back to the U.S., joined my frantic parents, and found out that it was the beginning of the Cuban Revolution; it was in all the U.S. newspapers." Robert and Agnes Blee were amazed that Nancy and Lefty had even been allowed to leave Cuba.

Once they had arrived safely in Miami, the Blee family, including Nancy, was relieved, but Lefty seemed unfazed by the experience. "She was a brave gal with a carefree attitude," Nancy remembers, "or so people believed.

She was not so cavalier really." This was a very different Lefty from the one who had struggled with night classes. This Lefty broke rules and courted danger. Nancy saw the difference and wonders aloud why Lefty was so different in Cuba. Many would likely call her brave when "she walked up to an armed soldier and asked for a picture, but it was more like naiveté. In the U.S. Isabel was also shy and not always sure of herself, but she tried [to be confident]; that's it, she tried. In Cuba with her family it was like she did not try." Rather than confidence, Nancy Blee sees childish rebelliousness. In fact, "It was like she became younger, less confident." As she had done when she returned to Cuba during the off-season, on this trip Lefty became that "little Cuba girl" who was shaped and controlled by Virtudes. Nancy had not seen that side of Lefty and did not anticipate the extent of Virtudes's influence or Lefty's determined rebellion against it. "It was very strange. On one hand she did not obey her mother. We walked into the middle of a revolution because she ignored her mother's instructions. But on the other hand Isabel became this petulant child."

One possible explanation for her behavior is that while Mr. Blee may not have realized it, Lefty had not wanted to return to Cuba and "the mess that was my family." During the AAGPBL off-season Lefty had been forced to return to her parents' home, and in 1957 she likely felt forced again. But she would never have said no to Mr. Blee. She understood he meant no harm in insisting she go, but for her that visit to Cuba represented a return to the insecurities of her childhood, and she simply acted out. "It was not the best way to handle it," she admits, "but I did not know how to say no. I did not want to be there, so I went and was bad to my mother." It would be another twenty-two years before Lefty would return.

In the years between 1957 and her final visit in 1979 Cuba and her family had changed drastically. On January 1, 1959, rebel forces led by Che Guevara seized control of the capital in Havana, and Batista fled the country. Just six days later, on January 7, Fidel Castro led some nine thousand rebels into Havana. Many police officers and Batista loyalists were tried and executed. Since Lefty was in the United States and out of harm's way, it is likely that her parents did not divulge many of the details about the revolution to her, but Nancy remembers that Lefty was worried about her parents, especially given her father's loyalty to Batista: "She always sent money to them since her dad had lost his job in the political situation. Isabel was very concerned about them as goods and essentials were very scarce and money was even more scarce." The strained relationship between the United States and Cuba intensified into the 1960s, making it even harder for Lefty to return to Cuba or to help her family. Lefty remembers, "My mother said to me, 'Don't come home. If you still believe in God, do not come back to Cuba. It is bad here.'"

The situation with her family, which Lefty learned about through letters, got worse. Lefty remembers with both sadness and anger that her brother was at odds with her parents and even fought with them about the ownership of the family home. "Tony said that Castro gave it to him because he fought for the revolution," she says. "My mother and father said no; this is their house. So they built a wall down the middle, and all of them—my parents and my brother and his family—lived in the house. It was a mess, and I was glad to be here, away from it all." Given the political and family turmoil of that time, it is no wonder that Lefty's mother discouraged her from returning or that Lefty had no desire to go.

The situation in Cuba may have made Lefty's decision to get a green card and become an American citizen a painful one. Lefty recalls that American citizenship had at one time been her mother's most important dream for her and one of the reasons she had sent her to play baseball. It was also true, however, that things had changed with the revolution. As much as Virtudes wanted Lefty to be in the United States and to be successful away from Cuba, she also wanted access to her only daughter. Nancy Blee remembers, "Isabel's mother was upset that she was going to become a citizen of this country." They were hearing all kinds of negative things about the United States at that time, and her mother was upset that she might never be able to see Isabel again." Lefty's parents were right to worry. As they expected it would, the revolution had a huge impact on Lefty and her family. Lefty knew that after the revolution she would have a hard time visiting her family, but despite the fears, she sought a green card and eventually American citizenship.

Lefty Alvarez began the process of attaining citizenship the same year she visited Cuba. With the help of the Blees, who sponsored her, Lefty first got a green card. Lefty had been living in the United States for twelve years at that point, had worked, and was in possession of a work visa, making this a fairly easy process. She was unaware of the struggles her countrymen endured when they sought American citizenship. She recognizes that baseball had been instrumental in getting her to the United States, noting, "I was told later that it was hard for Cubans to come here, but . . . it was okay for me because of baseball, I guess." At first Lefty laughs when it is suggested to her that baseball made it easier for her to become an American citizen. Then she stops and says, "Holy cow! I guess it really did, didn't it?" Lefty took advantage of the opportunity baseball had provided and became an American citizen.

As the Alvarez family expected, the relationship between Cuba and the United States worsened after 1959. The number of Cubans seeking American citizenship also rose. Between 1959 and 1962, 119,922 Cubans arrived in the United States. Initially these immigrants were from Cuba's elite. They were executives and owners of big businesses, sugar mill owners, representatives of foreign companies, and other professionals whose economic interests were threatened by the revolution.[4] They did whatever they needed to in order to escape from Cuba. Many were able to obtain U.S. immigrant, student, or tourist visas, while others entered the United States indirectly through countries such as Canada, where they applied for U.S. visas.[5] Between 1960 and 1961 roughly fourteen thousand unaccompanied minors arrived in the United States through a clandestine U.S. program code-named "Operation Pedro Pan."[6]

In 1960 Cuba and the USSR formalized ties, and Cuba began receiving Soviet aid, including oil and arms. American assets in Cuba were nationalized. In March 1960 President Dwight Eisenhower authorized the CIA to train Cuban refugees to overthrow Castro. The invasion did not take place during Eisenhower's administration, but President John Kennedy, needing to demonstrate his anti-Communist strength, authorized the mission. On April 17, 1961, fifteen hundred CIA-trained Cuban dissidents attempted to invade Cuba at Playa Giron. The mission, which became known as the Bay of Pigs invasion, was a categorical failure, and Castro used his victory to reaffirm his control over Cuba. Two days after the failed invasion Castro declared Cuba a socialist country, and he strengthened ties with the Soviet Union.[7] Within a year the United States and the Soviet Union were embroiled in what would become known as the Cuban Missile Crisis. In October 1962 an American spy plane spotted Soviet medium- and long-range missiles pointed at the United States, and from October 14 to October 28 the United States and the Soviet Union were in a tense standoff. After thirteen terrifying days in which Americans prepared themselves for nuclear war with the Soviet Union, Kennedy and Soviet leader Nikita Khrushchev negotiated and finally avoided war when the Soviets agreed to dismantle the weapons in Cuba and the United States agreed to do the same with its weapons in Turkey.[8]

During this very tense time between her two counties, Lefty outwardly seemed to pay little attention to the conflicts, but as Nancy Blee remembers, she did worry: "She never critiqued the U.S. or Cuba during those times, although she worried a lot about her family there and the fact that she could not go home by legal routes, which were closed from the U.S. to Cuba, even for a Cuban citizen." The attempted invasion of Cuba at the Bay of Pigs, the Cuban Missile Crisis, and the eventual American embargo of Cuba made it harder for Lefty to help her family, her primary concern. Despite the family struggles and Lefty's underlying anger at her family, she felt responsible for them: "I made it out of Cuba and had money so had to help them the best I could. It was hard, though, and I worried a lot. It made me very upset not knowing what to do for them. This difficulty added to my making other bad decisions."

Drinking alcohol to excess was one bad decision. Lefty wrecked a number of cars in this period and recalls once running off the road into a corn field: "I was driving, and Nancy was with me. I think I had been drinking some and just ran off the road into the corn field. I did not stop or try to get help. I just kept going in circles in that field until the farmer came out with his shotgun. Holy cow! I was scared. I finally just drove out and went on home." Nancy Blee also remembers that incident. "I have never been so scared in my life. Well, maybe when we were in the middle of the Cuban Revolution, but other than that, never," she says with a laugh." Over fifty years later as the two women remember those events, they both just look at one another, laugh, and shake their heads. "Holy cow!" Lefty finally says through the laughter. "Holy cow!"

Despite the laughter, Lefty has a lot of remorse. She remains thankful now that she did not kill herself or someone else while driving drunk and has a great deal of regret about that time when, as she says, she "was not living right." In that period she did not have her own home, and "wherever there was a friend, I would stay there," she recalls. "I actually never had a real home. You see [that is] how I used to be, just here and there, wherever I had a friend to stay with."[9] In the face of this crisis, when she was drinking heavily and sleeping on people's couches, Lefty found renewed strength. As she had done in the past, Lefty relied on the survival skills she had learned while playing sports. The lessons she learned while playing and the way she embodied those experiences, the physical memory of them, even influenced her during those "lost days." "When I had hard times," she says, "I remembered what it felt like being good, a rascal, a baseball player. Usually it was on those mornings when I woke up hung over and afraid about how I had gotten home. Wonder why I remembered it then?" All of us have coping mechanisms that emerge when we need them, often without our realizing what is happening. For Lefty it was her "sport self," as she calls it, that served that purpose. Her sport self reminded her when and where she was good, confident, *la pilla*. Memories buried deep in Lefty's psyche surfaced in the moments she needed them most.

That sport self was there for Lefty when another opportunity presented itself to her. While she was working at the Nine Mile, Lefty learned from friends that General Electric (GE) was a good place to work and could provide her with a secure future if she could get hired. Many of Lefty's friends worked at GE and were happy there, so Lefty decided to apply. She applied many times, but her poor English and lack of education got in the way. Even simple tasks like filling out the application were not straightforward for her.

Robert Blee worked at the GE plant as a manager, and Nancy Blee remembers that it was her father who finally helped to secure employment for Lefty. Lefty insists that it was she who landed the job all on her own. It is possible that both viewpoints are accurate—that Mr. Blee put in a good word for Lefty while her own tenacity, determination, and work ethic impressed the company. In any case Lefty's persistence paid off. She was finally hired in 1962 on her fourth try. "All that time I could hardly wait to get to General Electric," she says. "If my friends liked it, I knew it would be good for me." Her first position had her welding transformers and assembly units. From 1962 until she retired in 1999, Lefty worked on the line at GE.

In many ways the work at GE seemed made for Lefty, tapping into that sport-self-confidence. Her first position, as a welder, suited her. "I can do anything with my hands," she says, "like work on a car [or do] plumbing or carpentry." Responding to a question about where she learned these skills, Lefty says, "No one ever taught me; I learned on my own, like [with] baseball. I just always knew how to play, how to throw and catch. I think that helped me to do stuff with my hands; it feels the same to me." Lefty became a leader in her section. She was charged with the goal of finding better ways of doing the work and teaching new employees. She comments: "I enjoyed being leader at first and got along with everyone. But then I would get so mad when they made mistakes. I'd go home all worked up. I think I demanded too much."

Because of her dedication to the job, her aptitude for the hands-on work, and her ability to teach coworkers, Lefty was eventually asked to become a division supervisor. She recalls: "I even went and took classes and all that but then decided I couldn't do it. I could do this job, teaching somebody. I liked quality work but didn't like to be a foreman, writing things, keeping track of times, records. I didn't want an office job. I'm not made for that." These statements reflect the extent to which Lefty was anxious about her learning disability and likely embarrassed about her lack of education.

Because she lacked formal education and felt embarrassed by her strong Cuban accent, Lefty did not actively seek advancement at GE. "Just because of my accent people did not think I was intelligent," she says. "I could talk but my words were more or less backward—you know, mixed up—and they'd think I was dumb." Of course she was anything but "dumb," but the fear that others might think so kept her quiet and stuck in positions at GE that did not allow for advancement or much increase in pay.

Lefty's reluctance to move up in the company was also tied to her powerful need for security. There was a lot of competition within the workplace for better-paying jobs, but she kept her head down and did not get involved in any discussions about people who made more money. Because she stayed in the same type of job, she did move from division to division, and that, she says, "gave me security. I knew I was safe there." Unlike most workers at GE Lefty never got laid off, a fact she is very proud of and uses to "prove that I was in the right place."

Lefty's reluctance to seek promotion extended to a reluctance to support organized demands for equality. Attempts to get better pay for women at GE began in 1970, when salaried women workers at the GE plant in Erie fought important battles for workplace equality, including two strikes in 1974 and 1975. The workers demanded equal pay for equal work. The participants in these struggles were predominantly young women, and they were influenced by the ideas of the feminist movement, as well as their union's long-held principle of equality.[10] The union filed a grievance on behalf of its female members, demanding equal pay for equal work, but the company refused to budge. In October 1974 a four-day weekend strike that included twenty-four female employees took place. That was the first time women of GE had participated in a strike. According to the United Electrical, Radio and Machine Workers of America, the women picketed the Erie plant. As they returned to work and passed through the production areas, they were given a standing ovation by Local 506 members.[11] Eventually more and more women in different areas of the plant planned walkouts, and in the late 1970s a ruling against GE by the Equal Employment Opportunity Commission (EEOC) forced the company to abandon some of the policies that kept women from moving into higher-paying jobs. The company was also required to give upgrades and issue checks to a number of women workers who had experienced job discrimination, although the back pay did not fully compensate them for lost wages.[12]

Lefty was aware of the strike but did not act to support it: "[Women] thought they should make the same as men. I guess that's right. We should. But I heard about that trouble from my supervisor, and it scared me." Because she was so concerned about personal security, Lefty resisted the idea of labor organizing. She saw her work issues as personal ones. Typical of Lefty, she did not engage in any kind of "trouble at work," and even though these strikes took place in Erie and not Fort Wayne, she remembers being leery of anyone who was not simply grateful to be working: "There was a lot of jealousy about people who made more money, but I just didn't let things bother me. I did what I was told and was thankful I had a job." When asked if she thought she was discriminated against at GE, she is adamant that she was not. She does not remember if that strike had any impact on her salary in Fort Wayne, but it ultimately had an effect as the women from the Erie plant had set the stage for better pay and better opportunities for female workers at GE.

From 1962, when she was hired, until 1979, Lefty's life was centered on three things: working at GE, playing softball, and drinking. She was finally able to purchase her own home, a trailer on some property just thirty minutes from the Blees, but she continued to be lonely and therefore relied on alcohol to ease the pain. Interviews with Lefty include very little information about this period in her life. There are a few stories about drinking and mornings when she woke up with no idea how she had gotten home the night before or how her car had gotten wrecked. There are stories about playing softball and drinking with her softball friends. There are even discussions about her pride at maintaining her job at GE despite the drinking. But when pushed about her memories of those years, she simply shakes her head and says, "They are lost I think, lost in the bottle."

By the mid- to late 1970s Lefty was given a chance to return to Cuba. President Jimmy Carter had begun efforts to improve relations between the United States and Cuba. He lifted all restrictions on U.S. travel to Cuba, and in September 1977 Cuba and the United States each established an interest section in the other's capital. Relations continued to be strained, however, and the two countries struggled to reach an agreement on a relaxation of the U.S. embargo on trade. Carter's goal—to allow select medicines to be traded to Cuba—caused great concern among his political opponents.[13] In December 1978 ten members of Congress visited Cuba; as a result, the Cuban government released a U.S. business manager who had been accused of being a CIA agent in 1963. Later that same year fifty-five people who had been brought from Cuba to the United States by their parents returned to the island for three weeks. Also in December 1978 the two countries agreed upon their maritime borders, and the United States responded to a Cuban relaxation of restrictions on emigration by allowing Cuban Americans to send up to $500 to an emigrating relative.[14] Beginning on January 1, 1979, Cuban Americans could visit family in Cuba. Over the next year more than one hundred thousand Cuban Americans visited Cuba. Lefty was one of them.

Lefty wrote to her mother about the possibility of a visit, but despite the fact that Virtudes missed her terribly, she was not encouraging. "Do not come," she wrote. "It is bad here, worse than you can imagine." It wasn't just her worries about the political, economic, and social issues confronting Cuba. In many of her letters Virtudes wrote about how difficult it was for her living with Prudencio and Tony. Lefty says, "It was like she was their slave. She had to cook for them all the time and clean the house, even after working hard all day." Lefty was very upset with her brother and father but also understood how hard it could be to deal with her mother: "Sure, my mother had a tough character and was strong, and the relationship with all of the family was horrifying." Despite her mother's warning and the intense family difficulties, Lefty returned to Cuba in 1979. While, as always, Lefty felt ambivalent about returning, her sense of family obligation was stronger.

When Lefty arrived in Cuba, the welcome was anything but joyous as she recalls: "I got to my parents' house and had not even unpacked when my mother started screaming all sorts of things. She said my brother had tried to kill her. My brother overheard this and came into the room to defend himself. This was the welcome I received even before I could unpack." Lefty remembers that she was surprised that the house had a wall down the middle and that each of the two families lived on separate sides. She muses, "Both sides were very small, and I am not sure how my brother and his wife and kids could live in that small space. He insisted that the whole house was his, that Castro had given it to him. And my parents said, 'No. This is our house.'" After the revolution Castro had supplied some of his followers with houses, but those were likely his closest advisers. It is more likely that Tony was helped by the new housing reforms implemented after the revolution. In 1959 the government established its goal of providing each family with an adequate dwelling. The housing distributed by the government was property confiscated from people departing Cuba after the revolution.[15] In some cases houses were simply split down the middle with a wall to create two separate dwellings. It is possible that both Tony and Lefty's parents had a claim to the house, but neither would move an inch in that fight.

All of them wanted Lefty to take their side in the debate over the ownership of the house, but the core of their differences predated the political differences between Prudencio and Tony. Even years later Prudencio and Virtudes could not forgive Tony for having attempted to get Lefty into the shower with him when they were children. They continued to think of Tony as bad, and his support of Castro and his role in the revolution only solidified that assessment. During Lefty's 1979 trip back to Cuba it was as if no time had passed, and once again Lefty found herself in the middle of the family's political and emotional differences.

The trip brought into focus Lefty's conflicts with her brother. Tony, who was a block captain of the street and a man who demanded respect, successfully managed Lefty's time while she was there. He demanded that he be along for every visit to friends and neighbors, and he even kept Lefty from her nephew, Tony's oldest son, with whom he did not get along. Tony was feared in the neighborhood; Lefty is sure that he had killed people during the revolution. "Even the dogs on the street were afraid of him," she says. "If he walked down the street and someone had dogs and the dogs barked at him, he did not like it. He would go to the house and talk to the people. I do not know what he said, but the dogs did not bark again." Lefty was both frightened of him and angry that she let him keep her from spending more time with her parents.

While in Cuba, Lefty tried to learn about the relationship between Tony and her parents. It was for that reason that she wanted to talk to neighbors, but Tony would not allow it. She is convinced that he was afraid they would try to "brainwash her or ask too many questions," so he controlled every situation. He spent most of the time trying to defend himself, telling the story from his point of view. He even tried, with no success, to turn Lefty against her mother. Lefty summarizes: "I tried to be fair to my brother and even told my mother that I needed to forgive him. She was very angry and yelled at me, 'Don't you remember what he said about us? That we were lesbian?' Yes. He did say that because we slept together, but he is my brother." By the time Lefty returned to the United States, she was more confused and angry than before she went to Cuba. She wanted to forgive her brother but was also mad that he had kept her from the rest of her family. It was with a great deal of guilt and sadness that she left Cuba in 1979, the last time she saw her parents.

Upon her return from Cuba Lefty suffered a lot of sadness and guilt. Because Lefty had moved to the United States when she was so young, she did not know her mother as an adult. It took Lefty until after the 1979 visit to understand that she did not fully understand what her brother was talking about when he said their mother was not well, physically or mentally. Remembering that trip Lefty, recalls her grandmother asking her to never leave her mother because Virtudes would always need Letty to understand and take care of her: "That was not my mother's wish, though, so I left her. I feel guilty now. I never helped take care of my mother during her sickness. My brother knows. I was not there." The anguish caused by those memories can be measured by the increase in Lefty's alcohol consumption.

In the year following her trip to Cuba Lefty suffered some of the most intense depression and loneliness. She was still working at GE, and that provided her with some stability, but only the alcohol masked her pain. In that year she relied on her "sport self" in ways that she never had before: "I was nothing then—unhappy, scared, and not good at anything. I was glad to be in America but felt guilty for being here." As she had done throughout her life, whether consciously or not, Lefty allowed herself to rely on her sport identity to survive the difficult times. The ability to recognize and even embrace that part of her identity meant that she had at least one place where she was good, a success. She says, "Remembering that feeling made me remember what feeling good was like, and I was able to keep going until I got help with my drinking and my depression."

In what she remembers as a miracle, Lefty stopped drinking rather suddenly: "For almost twenty-six years I prayed to God for help, and it came on a day in 1980. I was forty-seven years old. He blessed me one night, and I never touched a drink again. I do believe it was a miracle." When pushed about that time, Lefty insists there was no event that caused her to simply stop drinking after all those years—no car accident or threat of losing her job—but she agrees that maybe it was the new knowledge that the one family she knew she could always count on, her baseball family, was about to reconnect, and Lefty never wanted to disappoint that family.

Lefty got word that some of the old ballplayers from the AAGPBL were trying to organize a reunion, and she knew what she had to do: "Be my best self. That's what they would expect." She notes that it was "first sports in general that gave me a life" and then "the AAGPBL that gave me the opportunity to be a success. I owed it to them and to myself to do better, so I did." Lefty quit drinking and prepared herself for the league's return to her life by being the very best "sport self" she could be. It was "almost like spring training," she says. Even after all those years and everything they had gone through, when it was time to reconnect to that time and to those women, Lefty got herself in shape, physically and mentally.

CHAPTER SIX

A League of Her Own

Finally someone noticed. Boy, did they notice!

LEFTY ALVAREZ

For thirty years Lefty worked alongside her colleagues at GE, but not until 1992 did any of them know about her baseball past. She played on the GE softball team, so they knew she played ball and that she was a good athlete. But no one knew she had been part of a professional women's baseball league or even that women had ever played professional baseball. It isn't that Lefty didn't try to tell her friends. "Even if I did try to talk about playing baseball," she remembers, "people would say, 'You mean softball'; women don't play baseball." Then again Lefty's GE colleagues were not alone in their ignorance of the AAGPBL. That same softball comment was repeated thousands of times to nearly every ballplayer who had tried to discuss her experience in the AAGPBL; eventually most of them, including Lefty, simply stopped trying. In fact most of the country was in the dark. With Major League baseball games broadcast on national television and a societal shift back to more traditional gender roles, the AAGPBL became a relic, unneeded and simply forgotten. For thirty years the players' contributions to baseball and to history were all but erased.

It wasn't only the public who forgot the league. Most of the players also lost contact with one another. That loss of contact with her former teammates was very difficult for Lefty. She knew there were some AAGPBL players in the Fort Wayne and surrounding areas, but, she says, "I just thought they would not want me to bother them," so she didn't reach out. It may have been that she was too ashamed. Lefty's life after the league ended did not measure up to what she believed the other players had accomplished. She struggled in ways that embarrassed her, and while she missed them, she also did not want her former teammates to know just how hard things were for her, so she did not make contact. Lefty also seems to have believed that her sense of personal indebtedness to the league was unusual. "I think it was different for many of the girls," she explains. "Maybe it wasn't that important for them. For some of them it was only about baseball, and when it was over, they moved on. It was not that way for me. Baseball was important to me, inside. *I am* because of the league and because of the friendship they gave me. Without sports I did not know how to act, how to talk. With baseball they showed me how."

But Lefty was not alone. Unbeknown her many players suffered from the same sense of loss that she did. In Chicago, former Peoria Redwing Terry Donahue remembers longing for those old friendships too: "Oh, I went on and had a good life after the league, but I sure missed those girls. I remember wondering if anyone else did." From California to New Jersey players wondered about their friends and teammates, and they longed for those old days. While many were able to replicate the feelings of closeness one feels on a team when they played softball or other sports, it wasn't the same. Lefty's old friend Jane Moffet, a very good college basketball player and eventually a high school principal in New Jersey, led a very successful life after the league ended. But even Moffet, who first scoffed at the idea of the players having a reunion, admitted that she too missed "the gals," over the years, "even that crazy Cuban." Out in Palm Springs, California, Maybelle Blair also longed to reconnect. Even though she had played in the league for only a year, she remembers, "Those girls were so important to me, in just that one year in the league. Isn't that funny?" Lefty was not alone in her desire to reconnect with her teammates, but unlike some of the others, she did not possess the confidence to make the reconnection happen. She had to wait until someone else did so.

Such longings would eventually lead the players back to each other. A first attempt to reconnect players came from former league officials Ed Des Lauriers and Arnold Bauer. Between 1962 and 1963 they attempted to find "our girls," the former players. Des Lauriers had been a business manager for the league. Bauer had worked not only as an usher and a statistician, but had also housed many of the players from the South Bend Blue Sox.

Bauer remembers that over the years he and his wife had "4 girls each year but often many of the girls came to our house for dinner after home games."[1] The strong connection between host families and ballplayers was not uncommon. As the Blees were for Lefty, for many of the players a host family were just that: family. And vice versa. The relationship between player and host family was special. The players were often treated like members of the family with all the benefits and responsibilities that entailed. They were expected to join the family for meals, attend church, and complete chores. Former Rockford Peach Shirley Burkovich remembers her host family very fondly: "Even though I don't remember a lot of details from back then, I sure remember those wonderful people." Given such close ties between the players and families, it is no surprise that it was Des Lauriers and Bauer who made the first effort to find the players.

In 1962 Des Lauriers and Bauer created a survey and sent it out to over four hundred former AAGPBL players.[2] The survey asked about the players' family lives: Were they married? Did they have children? Had they gone back to school or to work? The survey also inquired about the former players' continued interest in sports.

Lefty was thrilled to get the survey: "I didn't know people were thinking about it, and I guess I just thought that time was over for me. Then when the papers came from the league asking what we had been doing, I got excited." She wasn't alone. Des Lauriers and Bauer got 148 responses.[3] One common theme in these responses was the importance for each of the players of their time in the AAGPBL. And as it was for Lefty, sport continued to be important in many of the women's lives. A few of the players had become either softball or basketball coaches, and nearly all continued to play sports. For some it was recreational softball; for others it was tennis, volleyball, golf, bowling, or fishing. Lefty had far more in common with other former players than she had imagined.

After Des Lauriers and Bauer received the completed surveys, they compiled their findings and sent them to all the players who had responded. In some of the surveys respondents had mentioned the idea of a players' reunion and how they would love to reconnect with teammates. In the end most did nothing to make that dream happen. It may have been that in the prime of their lives, families and careers were the former players' focus rather than reconnecting with baseball. Or it may have been that, like Lefty, they didn't know how to make a reconnection happen. Lefty remembers: "I couldn't do anything. I didn't know how, but I sure wished someone would have got us all together." In that difficult period of her life she regretted "all that time" that she had lost with her league family.

In fact it wasn't until the late 1970s that players began to seek each other out in earnest. Perhaps it was because they were aging that they chose the 1970s to begin their reconnection efforts. Or it may have been the influence of the feminist movement, which had begun demanding equal rights for women and fostering a growing appreciation for women's history, that inspired the women to find each other. It was likely a combination of both. Either way, in 1978 Dorothy Kamenshek, a former Rockford Peach, along with Marge Wenzell from the Muskegon Lassies, visited former Fort Wayne Daisy June Peppas in Michigan. The visit was memorable because it was there that the three of them began asking, "Where is everyone? What are they doing now?" In an attempt to answer those questions, they decided that the first step was for Peppas, who owned a printing company, to send letters to all the former players for whom she had contact information. Unfortunately this list did not include Lefty Alvarez. Because she had not remained in contact with her teammates, few even knew how to find her.

Replies to the letters returned slowly, but they came, and it seemed that the interest was definitely there for some sort of league reunion. In January 1981 Peppas sent out a newsletter that consisted of one typed page. It was short, but the impact was powerful. She asked for more contacts and for the players to reach out to as many of their former teammates as they could find. By February 1981 Peppas had sent another newsletter; this time it went to 130 individuals, again not including Lefty. In this newsletter Peppas requested more information about former players and inquired about life after the league. The response was even greater than before, and another newsletter was sent out in March 1981. This version was longer and included an "In memory of . . ." section, more addresses, and pictures. Peppas included newspaper clippings from the days of the league and introduced the idea of a national reunion on a large scale. An edition of the newsletter came out nearly every month after March 1981, and for the players the journey back to each other began in earnest. A few of the former South Bend Blue Sox organized the first reunion for August 1981. At around the same time Peppas hosted a picnic at her home in Michigan and reported on it in the next newsletter: "We plan on lots more gatherings in the very near future." By September 1981 the overwhelming theme of the newsletters was the demand for a national reunion.

Lefty's isolation from this rediscovery finally ended that fall. The Fort Wayne Women's Bureau (where Lefty's friend Dona Schaefer worked) and the radio station WMEE sponsored an event called "Run, Jane, Run—Women in Sports."[4] "Dona got me involved," Lefty remembers. "Thank God she did that, huh?" The event was a celebration of women in all sports, including volleyball and softball. The final event, however, was a reunion of former Fort Wayne Daisies, who played a three-inning game against the Junior Daisies. It was a short game but likely the most important three innings of Lefty's life. "My goodness, it was fun," Lefty remembers. "We laughed and played like in the old days." The game seemed to bring Lefty back to the confidence and sense of self she had had as a ballplayer. As she puts it, "We had fun together, but we also showed off a little. We wanted people to see what good athletes we still were." At last Lefty was becoming part of the movement to reconnect former AAGPBL players.

That September weekend in 1981 was a huge success. June Peppas reported in the October newsletter that "the game drew about a 1,000 old and young Daisy fans who thoroughly enjoyed the game and wanted more. There were also many autograph seekers to be had. . . . I wonder if anyone else got up stiff on Monday morning?"[5] For Lefty it was "one of my happiest times. I felt like a rascal again," she says with a hearty laugh. The experience also went a long way toward eliminating the fears Lefty had had about bothering her teammates. Run, Jane, Run was the beginning of her path back to them.

The event was so popular that it became an annual mini-reunion for the members of the AAGPBL, an opportunity for them to reunite with their former teammates. Fortunately for Lefty and the other former players, that was only the beginning. The success of the Fort Wayne event gave new energy to the discussion of a national reunion. Sitting at a picnic table after that first reunion game, players Lib Mahon, Twi Shively, Mary "Wimp" Baumgartner, and Ruth Davis (a bat girl for the South Bend Blue Sox) got into a conversation about a national reunion. Some thought it would be too hard to do on a national scale, but Davis remembers saying, "Well, how hard can it be?" She volunteered to lead the way in organizing the reunion. In an interview with Merrie Fidler, Davis explained not only her motivation, but also the source of her strength:

> I think . . . perhaps that is the greatest legacy of the League, that it pre-
> sented a model for all of us growing up at that time that we could do
> whatever we set our minds to—because we didn't know that we couldn't.
> We saw women who were participating in a sport where women had
> never played before (professionally). We saw those same women go on
> to become pioneers in physical therapy, medicine, aviation, education,
> law. We saw some of them become rich, some dedicate their lives to
> the poor, to the church, and to humanity. The women who played in
> the League were not just great athletes; they were the best this country
> had to offer in so many ways. . . . I know that not everyone fell into that
> mold, but if I were a statistician, I'd bet that the greats outweighed the
> not so greats at a statistically higher rate than in the general public. [6]

Davis's "can do" spirit, along with Peppas's newsletter, made the organization of the reunion possible.

The first national reunion of the AAGPBL was set for July 1982 in Chicago. When Lefty had first arrived in Chicago thirty-five years before, she had been alone and overwhelmed by the size of the city, the cold weather, and her lack of English. This time Lefty entered the Chicago City Center Holiday Inn to a lobby filled with old friends, women with a shared history and a common goal of reconnecting the players of the country's only professional women's baseball league. Reports from Ruth Davis indicated that over two hundred reservations had been made in advance, and more showed former players up as the date drew near. As Davis wrote later to all the attendees, "It was a beautiful experience to be a part of the reunion of so many wonderful people. As we sat in the lobby, watching you enter the front door, many tentatively (wondering if anyone would remember?) we could see apprehension turn to absolute joy as names rang out and people enfolded each other in love that years and distance had not been able to diminish."[7] For Lefty that experience helped to squash any remaining worries about not being welcome by her former teammates. "They did not know me until I opened my mouth," Lefty remembers with a laugh. "As soon as I said, 'Hi,' they said, 'Lefty!'" After thirty-five years of being known as "Isabel," Lefty was part of that group again, "enfolded . . . in the love that years and distance had not been able to diminish," that of lasting friendship.

Yet the experience of seeing some of these teammates for the first time in nearly thirty years was difficult in one respect. Lefty remained embarrassed about not having gotten a formal education, and she carried a great deal of guilt about the years she had lost to alcohol. "I was ashamed that I did not do more [with my life]," she remembers. "They all did so much, but I guess I was okay for a little Cuban." The way Lefty demeans herself as a "little Cuban" is painful and speaks to a survival mechanism she has used throughout her life. By lowering people's expectations of her and diminishing her own, she could let herself off the hook when she did not measure up to some standard. But the reality is that this was a façade that covered deep insecurities. Her teammates were not aware of Lefty's fears, but they would not have mattered to them; they welcomed her with open arms.

The reunion was not all about simply reconnecting, however. It was a four-day affair that included a Chicago Cubs game, a golf outing, a boat tour, a jazz tour, a banquet, and "a huge activities room set aside by the hotel" for visiting and reminiscing.[8] The entire four days were chock full of fun and "getting to know each other as adults," Terry Donahue remembers. "We were just kids before; we had grown up apart, and now, amazingly, we still liked each other!" There was no doubt that for those in attendance that first national reunion was a very special time. "The lobby became the scene of the world's biggest love-in!" the newsletter crowed. "If it never happens again, it happened this once—a reunion not to be duplicated and always to be remembered in everyone's hearts—forever."[9]

The reunion was such a success that players vowed that they should continue to happen on a semi-regular basis. The next national reunion was scheduled for 1986 in Lefty's hometown of Fort Wayne. This time Lefty was determined to be involved in the organizing, so she joined an organizing committee made up of former players Dottie Collins and Wimp Baumgartner, former chaperon Helen Harrington, former manager Harold Greiner, and Lefty's good friend Dona Schaefer, who was well placed to help in her job with the Fort Wayne Women's Bureau. This work was extremely important to Lefty. Having missed her first opportunity to help get former players together back in the late 1970s, she was glad to have a second chance.

Lefty very clearly remembers the excitement and anticipation that seized the organizing committee. The plan was to have the reunion as part of that year's Run, Jane, Run event. "We would call each other and talk about plans. We met and worked with the radio station [WMEE] and the [Fort Wayne] women's bureau," Lefty says. "They helped us and were interested in our story. I was so excited I could not hardly sleep sometimes. Holy cow! We were excited." For athletes who play team sports the importance of being part of a team never goes away, even after the playing is over. For Lefty, ties to this committee meant she was part of that team again. Much of her excitement about this work was because of that fact.

Lefty does not have a lot of specific memories of her role on the committee. Her cloudy recall of her involvement was likely a result of the fact that the reunion was sandwiched between the deaths of her parents, Virtudes and Prudencio. In February 1986 Lefty's mother died at age seventy-four after a long and painful illness. Lefty had seen her parents for the last time during that difficult visit to Cuba in 1979. It had been clear to Lefty then that her mother was suffering, but as she said later, "I was so mad at my brother and my family for fighting that I did not pay attention. I should have gone back but I could not." Physically and even financially Lefty could have returned to Cuba, but emotionally she was unable to. Later she began to think of that as weakness and felt guilty about not being strong enough to be there for her mother.

The death of Lefty's mother must have been especially hard because of their complicated relationship. Virtudes had always been her champion and the person she credits with getting her into the AAGPBL and to the United States. But Virtudes could also be Lefty's harshest critic. She expected a great deal from Lefty: success, a life in the United States, and especially a respectable life. It didn't help Lefty's grief that she spent very little time leaning on or even communicating with her brother Tony back in Cuba. Their relationship remained strained. Virtudes's death could easily have derailed Lefty and sent her back to drinking. Fortuitously the 1986 reunion was on the horizon. Lefty was able to immerse herself in the AAGPBL, just as she had forty years before, when her family life had been so difficult. "What would I have done if she had died before?" Lefty wonders. "I do not know what would have happened to me." As it was, Lefty was able to lean on her rekindled relationships for support.

While the Fort Wayne committee was working on the second national reunion, a separate plan was in the making. Kelly Candaele, son of former player Helen Callaghan Candaele, with help from Kim Wilson, a filmmaker and Kelly's girlfriend, had begun work on a documentary they were calling *A League of Their Own*. When asked about their goals for the film, Kelly said that he wanted to "share a part of my Mom's life that I had heard about growing up and to honor her experience and achievements."[10] Candaele had begun taping interviews with his mother and with such California players as Faye Dancer and Thelma "Tiby" Eisen. He was excited to have so many other players in one spot at the Fort Wayne reunion and intended to do several more interviews while there. A Public Broadcasting Systems (PBS) station agreed to pay for Kelly to attend and to fly a production team to Fort Wayne to film the reunion. The fact that a film crew was at the reunion added to the excitement and gave many of the players a sense that perhaps what they had done so many years ago was important after all. Lefty remembers the buzz about the crew coming to the reunion, but she was not that impressed and was not interviewed for the project. "I just wanted to see my friends, laugh, and have fun like we used to," she says. "It turned out to be important though."

Indeed it did turn out to be important. But before that film's impact was felt, Lefty confronted another loss. Only a month after the reunion, on October 24, 1986, her father died. Her relationship with Prudencio had always been strained. She had come to believe that some of that was by her mother's design. Virtudes had had few positive things to say about Prudencio, especially after he lost his position with the Batista government. As noted, in letters to her daughter, Virtudes had written about how Prudencio and Tony mistreated her and made her wait on them like she was a servant. Lefty never confronted her father about those allegations, a fact she later regretted: "I should have asked about these things. I always just believed my mother, you know, because she took care of me, but I don't know, maybe I messed up. Now I do not know if my father was good or not." Many years after the death of her parents Lefty expressed guilt rather than grief when she talked about them. She wishes that she had visited them more or tried to help them more than she had. But almost in the same breath, Lefty claims that she did not openly grieve their deaths, did not cry on the shoulders of her friends. Those losses had to have had an impact on her, but late in her life, when the year 1986 was the topic, it was the reunion that dominated Lefty's conversation. This is not to argue that Lefty is callous or uncaring but that from an early age her family was often the source of pain and uncertainty. Her baseball family, the women she helped to bring to Fort Wayne, always provided the antidote, the escape she needed.

The Fort Wayne reunion had been a lifeline for Lefty. She continued to be part of the annual Run, Jane, Run events and maintained connections with former players Dottie Collins and Wimp Baumgartner. Through them she managed to maintain a connection with the league. "I saw a lot of Wimp and Dottie," Lefty remembers. "We saw some of the other girls too, but mostly they were my ties." Those friendships were important to Lefty, but in the latter part of 1988 and into 1989 her life got complicated again. She began having health issues, and there is no evidence that she attended the Scottsdale, Arizona, reunion in 1988.

In 1988, after years of doing the same work on the assembly line at GE, Lefty began having problems with her hands. The physical pain was intense. "The pain in my hands made it hard for me to work," she says. "I told the foreman about the situation, and he sent me to the nurse. I had to go to her a lot, but she could not help. [The foreman] told me that if I could not do the job, he did not have a job for me." As she had done her entire time at GE, Lefty did not question his authority. Instead one day at work she saw a posting for a position she knew would be less repetitive, thus easier on her hands. The job paid less and required that she work second shift, but afraid of unemployment, Lefty made the change. Eventually she was diagnosed with carpal tunnel syndrome. Although her new position may have been easier on her hands, it still inflamed Lefty's condition.

These setbacks took a huge emotional toll on Lefty. Finally even the nurse she saw for her hands noticed something was wrong. Lefty recalls: "She noticed I was acting different, so she took action to help me. She said, 'We have someone who can help you,' so they find out I [was suffering from] depression. They sent me to a therapist during the day, and I worked second shift. They gave me Prozac, and I never missed a day of work that whole time." Despite the physical and emotional pain she suffered, Lefty's pride in her strong work ethic shined through.

It was in the middle of this diagnosis of depression that Lefty's brother insisted on visiting the United States for the first time. Tony wanted to take advantage of an opportunity to leave Cuba. By 1989 Cuba's economy was in terrible shape. The Soviet Union, which had effectively subsidized the Cuban economy since the 1960s, collapsed that year, leaving Cuba with intense economic hardship. With the Soviet collapse Cuba lost more than 85 percent of its trade and had to search for other markets to replace the loss.[11] Cuba's economy declined by 35 percent between 1989 and the early 1990s.[12] Because the Soviets were the primary source of Cuba's fuel supplies, Cuban homes and businesses suffered daily power blackouts. The public transportation system all but stopped, and food became scarce. Hoping it might help the Cuban economy, Castro allowed for more travel between Cuba and the United States. Like all Cubans, Tony was suffering, and because Castro had loosened travel restrictions, he saw an opportunity to escape the difficult time in Cuba.

Lefty wondered later if there wasn't another reason for her brother's visit. She thought that maybe because things were so bad in Cuba, he wanted to see how Lefty lived: "Maybe he wanted to come here for good, bring his family and stay with me. I don't know." Whatever his reason, Lefty, struggling to deal with her mental and physical health and with the change in jobs, begged her brother not to come. The mere thought of his trip caused her great mental anguish: "I could not forget all that had happened when

I was a girl and how my mother tell me that my brother was no good." This comment makes it seem as though Lefty had no active will in how she dealt with her brother. It is true that Virtudes tried to sway Lefty's feelings about Tony, but Lefty also had reason to mistrust him, and mistrust him she did. Still in the end, he was her brother, and she simply could not refuse him.

Tony came to Fort Wayne in late 1989, but Lefty does not remember how long he stayed. It likely felt much longer to Lefty than it really was because later she remembered that his visit was as bad as she had thought it would be. Lefty's memories of Tony and his attempts to get her into the shower with him when she was a child rose to the surface as she nervously anticipated his visit: "I was still having trouble at work, and then at home I had to worry about him. What was he doing? I tell you I was afraid and locked the door in my bedroom. That was lunatic of me to do that, but so many things I could not forget." Given their past it makes perfect sense that Lefty would be afraid with Tony in the house. The most important part of the visit for Lefty was its ending. She was so happy when he left that the very day she took him to the airport, she stopped taking Prozac: "I thought I did not need to take any more pills. I still had bad times because of things I did, but that was the only time [I took pills] for depression. When my brother left, I felt happy. I started to think about other things again and did not have to just remember the bad."

The end of 1990 was a bittersweet time for Lefty. She felt guilty that she and her brother were not close and that she did not trust him, but she was also glad he had returned home and she no longer had to live in the same house with him. Her hands were better as a result of the new job, and her depression had lifted. She had not focused on the league in the few years after the Fort Wayne reunion, but as in the early 1980s, the league was about to change her life again.

At the Fort Wayne reunion in 1986, members began work to create the All-American Girls Professional Baseball League Players Association.[13] The AAGPBL PA would provide an organizational structure and give form to the now growing number of former players who had been reached by June Peppas, Dottie Collins, and others. The first official meeting of the newly formed players association was in May 1987 at Fran Janssen's home in South Bend, Indiana. The association became the public face and force of women's efforts to gain recognition for the league. At that meeting ideas were batted around, but everyone agreed that they should go for the top: recognition by the National Baseball Hall of Fame. This would ensure that the AAGPBL would never be lost to history again.

The idea was first floated in 1986 in the wake of excitement about the documentary. "Pretty fantastic, huh gals??" the newsletter declared. "We will be immortalized on celluloid for the future! . . . Perhaps a film on the AAGPBL might be the trumpet to topple the 'Walls of the Great Hall of Fames of Baseball! . . . Where does it say 'Men's Baseball Hall of Fame?'"[14] During the 1988 Scottsdale reunion the players began in earnest the push for recognition by the Baseball Hall of Fame (located in Cooperstown, New York), and such recognition became a priority for the women. Lefty remembers: "They were determined to get in there. I liked how they fought for us. Holy cow, they were stubborn!"

The women worked as a team to accomplish their goal. Players wrote letters to the Hall of Fame, contacted its president and curators, and sought to ascertain the amount of memorabilia that still existed for donation to the Hall. After a great deal of negotiation (and stubbornness) their efforts paid off. Ted Spencer, the Hall of Fame's curator who had begun communicating with representatives of the league in 1986, entered negotiations to get the AAGPBL players recognized by the Hall. Spencer assured the group that the Hall of Fame wanted to do an exhibit or display of some kind. Many league members did not want a display, nor did they want to share an exhibit with other women in baseball. They wanted the entire league to be inducted into the Hall as an honorary member, with a ceremony and full recognition. Maintaining that the Hall could not induct a whole league, as it went against its historical mission, Spencer proposed a compromise. There would be a "Women in Baseball" exhibit, as well as an unveiling and ceremony to honor the women. After a great deal of discussion and disagreement, the membership agreed to this proposal, and a date was set for the league's recognition by the National Baseball Hall of Fame.

One hundred and fifty former players from the AAGPBL and countless friends and family members met in Cooperstown on November 3, 1988, for the three-day event. Dottie Collins and Hall of Fame president Howard Talbot pulled the cord to unveil the "Women in Baseball" exhibit. As Ted Spencer remembered years later, "Here's a day where we have 400 people. That's what we'd have on a Saturday in November, 400 people. The place was packed, and they sang that song all day long. . . . And this museum had never had that much noise! It was great. . . . To me it changed the whole direction of the museum because it brought home how important the game is culturally."[15]

After the induction there was a lot of interest in the women and their league, significantly from a popular Hollywood film director, Penny Marshall, who had heard about the Hall of Fame display and celebration and decided to attend. After Marshall saw the documentary *A League of Their Own*, she secured the rights from Candaele and Wilson and began work on turning the documentary into a feature film that she would also call *A League of Their Own*. "Hidden in plain sight behind sunglasses and a baseball cap," she attended many of the events that weekend and left with the determination to do a movie about these women. As she explained it, "One day I saw a documentary on the All-American Girls Professional Baseball League of the 1940s. It was about a group of courageous women who were recruited to play baseball when the young men who played ball had gone off to fight World War II. I chose to direct *A League of Their Own* because I thought it was a story that needed to be told, and told with accuracy, inspiration and humor."[16] Auditions took place throughout 1989 and production on the film began in 1990. Several problems arose in the early stages of filming, including a record heat wave in the Midwest that summer. But by October of that year the filming was well under way. Throughout the summer and fall of 1991 the cast and crew of the movie worked long hours to complete the movie. In October they arrived in Cooperstown to film the movie's final scenes.

Since she had been part of the early reunions and was "in the loop about league things," Lefty knew that Penny Marshall had purchased the rights to the documentary *A League of Their Own*. She also knew when filming started and even kept up with the progress of the film. When word went out that the director wanted original players for those final scenes, Lefty headed for Cooperstown: "I just decided to go, so I took the time and I went to Cooperstown." Because of that decision Lefty ended up appearing in the film.

At the end of the Hollywood version of *A League of Their Own*, the ballplayers return to the Hall of Fame for a reunion game and recognition by the Hall. Lefty was one of several AAGPBL ballplayers who participated in that portion of the movie. On the screen a busload of former players arrives in Cooperstown. The bus pulls up to the entrance of the Hall of Fame, and Lefty, along with other players, exits the bus to find a huge welcome banner hanging over the entrance. Lefty remembers having fun with the filming. "They told me to get on that bus. Now, smile and walk off the bus. I did that, and now I am a movie star," she says with a laugh. She especially appreciates that the scene had them traveling. "That part of the movie, that was part of us," she recalls. "We were all together. We always traveled by bus. We always had so much fun; we were like family."[17] Lefty's scene was very brief, but the smiling, happy woman that beams on that screen was Lefty. Not Isabel, but Lefty, the ballplayer and the trailblazer.

The production completed filming on October 31, 1991, coincidentally Lefty Alvarez's fifty-eighth birthday. Lefty returned to Indiana, where she kept it to herself that she had a role in a movie. This had everything to do with her years of silence about being in the league. "I do not know why," she says. "Before, when I told people I had played baseball, they corrected me. They thought because I was Cuban I was confused, so they said, 'No, you mean softball.' So I just stopped talking about it." She had no reason to think a bit part in a film would get a different response. Then on July 4, 1992, *A League of Their Own* opened, and it opened the eyes of the world to the women who had played professional baseball. Interest in the league grew, and finally, after nearly forty years, women's professional baseball reentered the American consciousness. The days when most people did not even know that such a league had existed were over. The ballplayers became celebrities wherever they went.

Even with national attention on the league, it was a while before Lefty was able to reap any benefits from being "one of those ballplayers." In part this was because despite participation in the reunions, her part in the movie, and her reconnection to the league, Lefty still struggled with depression.

When she did talk about the league or the film and when people told her she was mistaken about her own history, her response was to get sad: "When people said no, you did not do that, play baseball, it was hard for me. I got more sad because they did not believe me." But it also made her increasingly angry, even defiant: "I knew the truth, and it made me proud. So I got mad. I decided to tell everyone I was one of those girls who played, and I did not care what they thought. It made me feel like I did when I was young. You know, that old rascal I was before. So I told them and then just smiled." Eventually the film backed her up: "One day I said to some people, 'You know that movie about the girl ballplayers? I was one of them.' They did not believe me at first until some people saw the movie; then they said, 'Hey, I saw you in that movie.'" Lefty was glad to be vindicated and even happier that she could talk about that time and openly relive it and its importance in her life.

Once Lefty was finally able to embrace her past as a professional baseball player and share it with others, the connection to that time was strengthened for her. During all those years, when the memories of playing baseball were less clear, so was her life: "When it was happening, when I drank and after I lost my way from baseball, I did not know who I was. I was a worker at GE, a Cuban, but not Lefty. People called me Isabel. I lost Lefty until the reunions, and when they said, 'Hi, Lefty,' I was so happy again. And then there I was on the movie screen. Lefty. Holy cow!" It is not an overstatement to say that seeing herself in that movie, alongside those women, proving to the world that she was one of them, was quite literally also the reunification of Lefty.

Many of Lefty's teammates had similar experiences when the movie came out, and they often share those stories at reunions. Even longtime friends of players did not know there had been a baseball league for women and certainly did not realize they were in the company of professional ballplayers until the movie made those players famous. Their friends did not understand the significance of the league to World War II history, to women's history, or to baseball history. For many young women, especially those who played baseball and softball in the years before the passage of Title IX, this film was a lifesaver. They saw for the first time that they were part of a larger history of women in sports, that they were not the only ones.

This movie was life altering for many girls and women who loved the games. It encouraged and empowered those girls and became the foundation for a movement in women's baseball that continues today.

For Lefty and her teammates, however, it was simply about time. Lefty's friend Terry Donahue argued until the end of her life that if it had not been for the movie, "we would have all been dead and gone and no one would have ever known about us." Donahue remembers how it was for them after the movie's release:

> We were overwhelmed really. We couldn't believe that we were getting all of this attention. Because any time you mention that movie, people go crazy. I think we were really overwhelmed and so excited. Well even now I don't think that it's changed much since the first time it came out. [I] mention to somebody that [I've] played, and, you know, they will see my [league] ring. I might be paying a bill or doing something, and I'll say, "Have you heard of A League of Their Own?" and you tell them that you've played; they just get so excited. It's incredible.[18]

That shared experience also forged bonds among the former players. One immediate impact of the film for Lefty was the strong friendships she formed with a group of former players she had not known back in the 1950s but who, like her, became very involved in the players' association after the film's release—players like Donahue, Maybelle Blair, and Shirley Burkovich. She looked up to them and talked with both pride and awe about what they did with their AAGPBL fame. Blair and Burkovich spent years traveling around the country, encouraging girls to play and demanding that they be allowed to do so. Donahue was popular on both the American and the Canadian stages. She used her experiences in the league as a Canadian to talk about the importance of sports in both countries. Lefty also admired her old friend Jane Moffet, who became one of the most outspoken and fearless leaders in the field of women's sports in the country.

All of these women's lives changed once the world realized who they were. For many, fame opened doors to travel, writing, and public speaking. To some, the idea of writing a book, speaking in public, or being interviewed for television or radio had seemed farfetched. After the release of the movie, however, they could engage in such endeavors. Most dealt well with their newfound popularity and even flourished because of it. Lefty had a harder time getting used to her celebrity status. Because she was so self-conscious about her accent and because she simply never saw herself as worthy, she resisted the limelight for as long as she could. "I've always been shy," Lefty says. "I never wanted to talk to people, but now, holy cow! People want to know my story all the time. So now I told them." She most certainly did. In Fort Wayne, where Lefty has lived since her playing days ended, she has been honored by the city, the mayor, the rotary club, the Northern Indiana Historical Society, and the Waynedale Lions Club, among many other organizations. Lefty has been the grand marshal of several parades and was the subject of a short documentary about her life, *Latin Nights: The Baseball Journey of Isabel Alvarez.*[19] "I could never do those things before. It was like a miracle," she says with a laugh. "I don't know. Maybe I just did not care anymore what people thought about my accent or me. Maybe I just got smarter; yes, that is probably it." She may not have gotten smarter, but Lefty redeveloped a level of self-confidence that she had not experienced since her playing days. Once Lefty saw the women's story on the movie screen—how strong and capable they looked—she admits that it felt good to be "reminded of how that felt. I saw how lucky we were, so I thought I should get better at telling the story. I think I have." She has gotten better at telling her story, and it seems every time she does, the significance of baseball to her survival is more evident. Perhaps practice and the experience of telling her story is the reason for that clarity, but she thinks, as I do, that it is the wisdom of age and her ability to better understand "her sport self" and just how important that part of her is to the story of her life.

One by-product of Lefty's newfound fame was that she found herself in a role she had never expected to be in: role model. After the release of the movie and the growth of the players' popularity, young girls began looking up to them, idolizing them, and seeking them out. Lefty was very uncomfortable with this role as well. Despite how much her confidence had grown over the years, Lefty still did not think she measured up to the other players. She laughs when asked if she thinks she was a role model. She responds: "For what? No education, no English, and bad driving? A lot of the players made something of themselves, you know; [they] became doctors and teachers. They are the ones who are role models." Lefty did not see herself as a role model, but she most certainly was one. She may not have been the best player in the league or the most successful after the league, but despite a poor education, a language barrier, and financial difficulties, Lefty not only survived in a foreign country, but she also became a productive citizen of that country. She found gainful employment and overcame alcoholism and the difficulties of a painful family life. Lefty found her way back to her teammates, and together they showed the world the importance of sport to the lives of women and girls. Despite her own accomplishments and the literally hundreds of times Lefty spoke to classes, was interviewed, or was written about, she plays down her status as a role model. She is very quick to point, with great pride, to the other players who "really did something with their lives [like] help other girls to play sports."

In Lefty's eyes stories about other players and their accomplishments are not just about those individuals and do not reflect only on the women whose names are mentioned. She feels these stories represent what they all did together: "You know what the song says, 'All for one, one for all.' That was how we were when we were a league, and now we are still that way. These people make me proud." When pushed to discuss her own accomplishments, she shrugs and says, "Have you heard what Blair and Shirley are doing?" Shirley Burkovich and Maybelle Blair (known to her teammates as Blair) recognized that the fame that came to them after the release of the movie provided them with a unique opportunity to talk about sports—not only the importance of playing, but also the ways in which sports help to further educational opportunities for girls. Shirley sums up:

We [Shirley and Maybelle] started working with other ex-Major League ball players on free clinics for girls and boys. The clinics used to be strictly for boys. Then . . . a group of us [including] some ex-Dodgers and ex-Angels . . . put together this group called Sports Educators of America . . . in the Southern California area. We would go out and do these free baseball clinics for the kids, and we would try to incorporate education and sports, telling the kids that education was just as important. If you ask the kids, "Who wants to be a Major League ballplayer?" everybody raises their hand. So then you say to them, "All right. There are seven hundred positions in Major League baseball. What if you don't make it? Then what? So we tell them that they've got to have something to fall back on, and we start stressing education ... to encourage them to stay in school and have a backup just in case they don't make it in the baseball world. I can always relate to that because that's what happened to me. I thought baseball was always going to be my career, and I didn't plan for anything else. Fortunately I got a job at the telephone company.

Young people all over the country have taken the women's message to heart, and that makes Lefty very proud. "Showing how important sports are is a good thing," Lefty says, "and [it is] one way we can help the younger girls."

Using the platform provided to them by the movie, the former AAGPBL players worked to encourage and educate girls. For many that was a natural reaction to their fame and a responsibility they took very seriously. Lefty and her teammates helped the cause of women's sports in the 1990s and beyond. They made access to sport a cause worth fighting for when they showed the world just how sport could impact girls if they were given a chance to play. Their lives will forever be changed. They will learn to win and lose, to have confidence in themselves, and, as Lefty's own life demonstrates, learn to rely on the skills and perseverance sports teach them.

It was not only the players' on-field experiences that influenced young people, however; it was also the educational and professional successes of the players following their departure from the league. These demonstrated to new generations that the traits developed and refined on the playing field could also benefit young girls in academic and professional pursuits. They showed that being athletic could lead to the development of confidence, independence, and autonomy, which could then be applied to multiple aspects of life. The players' stories illustrated both the physical and social importance of women's sports. Despite Lefty's resistance to the tag, such stories also gave to future generations a visible group of strong female role models.

Lefty is quick to point out that the years after the movie came out and after the National Baseball Hall of Fame recognized the AAGPBL players were not all about social responsibility. The former ballplayers knew and understood their place in the lives of girls, and that work on behalf of youth sports was rewarding, but to many, including Lefty, those things were just a bonus. Working together as a team, just like they had done on the diamond years before was Lefty's greatest joy. "What we did because we were famous was important," Lefty asserts. "But really for me what matters is that we are together. Whatever we are doing does not matter. Just that we are together." Those connections continued and strengthened once Lefty retired from her job in 1999.

After thirty-three years Lefty retired from GE. She was sixty-six years old. Lefty remembers only a small celebration when she left GE for the last time: "I just left like I worked. I kept quiet and did what I was supposed to do." She did not appear to be sad about leaving the job she had had for so many years; she was excited and "ready to be an All American full time." By this time the league's popularity was at a peak, and more and more opportunities arose for former players. Lefty had even more time and mental space to reconnect with the league and to reflect on the significance of it to her life. The result was a rededication to her teammates, who, in her words, "are the only ones who know Lefty. Isabel is someone else, sometimes a sad lady. Lefty, the ballplayer. That's who they know and who I am because of them."

Lefty embraced her newfound fame and became a local celebrity in Fort Wayne. Much of her time was spent working with community organizations and participating in league events. "I was so happy to have the time and that I did not have to worry about work," she says. "If someone wanted me to go to speak or something, I went." Because the former players got so much attention, archives and museums sought their memorabilia, and Lefty, a self-proclaimed "pack rat," started to realize the full impact of what they had done and of the historical importance of her collection. When the National Baseball Hall of Fame or the Northern Indiana Historical Society asked for donations of artifacts, Lefty had plenty. She donated some but kept most of her collection. In retirement she continued to collect stories, pictures, scrapbooks, and even uniforms. "It was important to keep all that," she says. "It is your life, so you keep things. I did not keep many things from my

Cuba life—some baseball things, but not from that life. That's funny how I did not think to keep those things." Later Lefty remembered that much of the correspondence between her and friends while she was in Cuba during the off-season, including pictures and other artifacts of her life there, was lost when a suitcase she was carrying from Cuba back to the United States was lost by the airline. She didn't seem too upset about those losses, saying, "My memories of that are enough."

From 1980 onward women from the AAGPBL reestablished themselves as family. They reconnected in reunions and, as noted, created a players' association that continues even today. They inspired a major motion picture that remains the highest grossing sports movie in history. They shared their stories and their passion for baseball with anyone who would listen, and the result was a new movement in women's sports. They remain celebrities wherever they go. Their legacy is important to the story of baseball and to women's history, but after all these years the players, to a person, will say that their greatest legacy is the ties they have to each other. Lefty is adamant that they are not "just family in the way that some people say they are family. We have a bond that no one else knows. When one of us dies. it is hard because there will never be any more of us." In 2008 Lefty's longtime friend and Fort Wayne Daisy Dottie Collins died. Lefty and a few other former players and fans of the league attended her funeral. At the end of the service Lefty stood and began singing the league song: "Batter up! Hear the call. The time has come for one and all. To play ball." At Lefty's insistence a few of the other former players stood to join her, but it was Lefty who led that tribute. She says, "It was the right thing to do, to sing our song for her. I know some were embarrassed, but I do not care about that any more. I learned that does not matter in these things." What matters to Lefty is respect and the lifelong commitment that each of her teammates has for one another.

The league reunions continued, and Lefty attended every one until 2013. That year she began suffering from dementia and was unable to make the trip. When word spread that Lefty was not coming, there was a genuine sadness among the attendees. Many offered to drive to Fort Wayne and get her and let her stay with them for the duration of the reunion. Despite the encroachment of dementia, Lefty was still Lefty. She refused that kind of help and insisted that she would either make it on her own or not at all. Lefty did not make the trip from Fort Wayne to Chicago and did not attend another reunion until 2015, when a caretaker took her to South Bend. "She walked into the lobby of that hotel, and you would have thought a movie star had walked in," says Maybelle Blair. "Everyone hugged her, and even though she did not recognize all of us, she smiled and laughed as if she did. You know she used to get lost a lot, and we all laughed at her for it. But she always seemed to have faith it would all work out. I couldn't help thinking about that when I saw her in South Bend. To see her you'd think she was mentally lost, but I don't think she was ever more found than in that moment."

Epilogue

I don't know why you want to write my book. I'm not important. No one cares about what I did. I was not the best player, had no education, and didn't speak good English. I am just a little Cuban.

LEFTY ALVAREZ

Since my first contact with her in 2003, I watched Lefty interact with her teammates and with a public who always wanted to hear more about her life. It took many of the years since that first meeting to convince her that her story was worth telling, but once she agreed Lefty, opened her heart and her life to me. I was privy to the darkness of her years in Cuba, the struggle she went through making a life in the United States, the pain of alcoholism, and the rebirth she experienced when the AAGPBL players reconnected in the 1980s. In every tale there was a thread that I did not even notice until I sat down to write her story: pride.

Despite her stories of mental abuse and financial struggle, despite the pressure she felt from her mother to make something of herself, and despite the political differences between her brother and father in the "un-Christian country" that Cuba became, Lefty has pride in her Cuban heritage. "I was not a fan of Castro and do not like what he did to my country, but, you know, we are a proud country," she says. Even after becoming a citizen of the United States, Lefty never stopped being proud of her Cuban heritage. "Especially," she says with emphasis, "I am most proud of our sports history. I think I am part of that too." As the girl who did not give up a hit in that first game in Havana Stadium in 1947 and who turned baseball into a career in the United States, she most certainly is part of that history.

Many of my conversations with Lefty about her early life in Cuba were personal in nature, including stories of fear and sadness. Her anxiety over school and about the plans her mother made for her dominated most of Lefty's stories about her childhood. But in nearly every story there was an aside. "Oh, and then I played marbles on the street with my brother," she would say, or, "Oh my goodness, I was always out climbing trees or playing baseball in the neighborhood. I was good." With every difficult story, she shared a little piece of her "sport self" too because even when relaying her darkest fears, she had to show at least one thing that made her proud. Lefty did not recognize that pattern either, and certainly turning to those sports memories was not a conscious act, but it demonstrates her reliance on them. It also helps explain why, when speaking of her pride in her Cuban origins, she emphasized having been part of Cuba's sporting heritage. Lefty put an even stronger point on this fact when she insisted that I include a timeline of Cuba's sports history and baseball history in this book.

Lefty was also proud of her time in the AAGPBL and the impact it had on young women. She had, after all, had an active part by helping organize league reunions, participating in filming the movie *A League of Their Own*, and spending much of her retirement speaking to audiences about the league's legacy. Lefty willingly shared her personal baseball story and has been the topic of documentaries, articles, and chapters of books about the league. Nonetheless, it was difficult for Lefty to think of herself as someone worthy of a legacy, and she would resist the idea that she should sing her own praises. When I asked her, "What do you want your legacy to be?" she was more often than not vague and dismissive. But somewhere deep inside she knew her story was important and that she had every right to be proud of that story. That is likely why she amassed a very large collection of Cuban and AAGPBL baseball artifacts and memorabilia.

Lefty saved much from her baseball life through pictures, uniforms, scrapbooks, game programs, jackets, gloves, shoes, and original correspondence between herself and the AAGPBL. She initially told me that her collection was a result of her pack rat tendencies. Later she seemed clearer about its importance to the overall story of women's baseball in Cuba and the United States. "Well, yes, maybe our story is important," she said. "At first I just thought I wanted to give this stuff to them," she explained ambiguously. It wasn't until later that I realized that the "them" to whom she was referring were the girls of today. Once I understood what she meant—that in essence this was for them to enjoy, learn from, and build on—this piece of her legacy and the ways in which she was able to demonstrate her pride in it began to take shape for me.

Lefty's memorabilia colorfully illustrate stories about her past and about the history of women's baseball. The uniform style of the Estrellas Cubanas, which was very similar to that of the AAGPBL, shows that Cuban organizers had connections to the league. It reminds us that even though baseball had been popular in Cuba for decades before the AAGPBL came to play there, organized women's baseball emerged, in part, because of the league's influence. Included in her collection are also publicity posters from the Latin American tour—for example, a poster that describes the March 13, 1949, game in Puerto Rico between the "Cubanas and the Americanas" as featuring "La 'premier' Cubana, Myra Marrero" and the "Renombrada [renamed] Pitcher Americana, Annabelle Lee."[1] Such posters, advertising the teams and touting the superb level of play, demonstrate how the AAGPBL and the Latin American Feminine Béisbol League worked together to create interest in and opportunities for women's baseball in both North and Latin America. Placing Lefty's Cuban artifacts within the context of the time, we get a clearer picture of Cuban women's baseball and its connection to American women's baseball.

A more complete picture of Lefty, the baseball player, also emerges. When Lefty reminisces about listening to baseball games on the radio with her mother, we get a sense of the two women as fans. But when we see the physical artifacts of that time—the homemade baseball, the old uniforms she wore, the posters, and even her socks—a more vibrant picture of Lefty, a Cuban baseball player, comes into focus. From her playing the game with baseballs made of old cigarette packs to proudly wearing the "actual uniform of Cuba," Lefty's early connection to baseball is vividly illustrated.

The bulk of Lefty's collection is made up of artifacts from her time in the AAGPBL. Included are numerous uniforms, jackets, shoes, and a glove, all used while she was a player in the league. There are also copies of the annual contracts she signed with the league. These artifacts, saved from her life in American baseball, allow us to see Lefty's transition from Cuban to American professional baseball player. Through this collection we can also explore the role of immigrants in the league. As one of only sixty-five women who immigrated to the United States to play baseball with the AAG-PBL, Lefty's story about immigration offers an important perspective. The contracts, correspondence, and papers she saved help us to understand the immigrants' experience in the league.[2] They also help us to map out Lefty's transition from Cuban to American citizen. In her contracts we can read the league's rules about visas and the necessity for each player to return to her home country after the season ended. There are copies of the citizenship study book Lefty used when preparing to become an American citizen and, finally, there are her citizenship papers. Lefty preserved pieces of her Cuban life and her life in the AAGPBL, and together they tell the story of immigration, of baseball, of perseverance, and of survival.

No element of Lefty's collection is more revealing, or entertaining, than her photographs. From pictures that show a beautiful, smiling baby Isabel to staged photographs with her brother Tony, we get a glimpse how Virtudes Álvarez wanted the world to see her children. In the professional action shots of Isabel playing the socially acceptable sports of volleyball, tennis, and fencing, we see Virtudes's attempts to frame her daughter's class status. Also included are early pictures of Lefty, the baseball player. She is featured in the Estrellas Cubanas uniform during the 1949 Latin American tour. After that year the pictures are very AAGPBL-centered. There are shots of Lefty playing in the league, friends from the league, and Lefty in the hospital as she recovered from the career-ending knee injury. There are, however, no pictures of her time back in Cuba during the offseason. Why there are no pictures of her time back in Cuba is not known, but that is not the only gap in her photograph collection. From 1954 until around 1980 there are no photographs. But starting that in 1980 suddenly there is an abundance of pictures of a smiling Lefty and her former teammates. It is clear from these photographs of Lefty playing in the Run, Jane, Run games that this was a happy period in her life. When asked about the gap in photographs between 1954 and 1980, Lefty responds, "Well, who takes pictures when they aren't proud? I was happy and proud sometimes and sometimes not."

These photographs show better than anything else the importance of Lefty's sport self to her overall happiness.

Whether through artifacts such as baseballs and uniforms, archival material such as publicity posters and contracts, or photographs, Lefty's collection covers years of baseball history and Cuban history. It is significant that it also documents her place in the history of both. As she maintained many times, Lefty was proud to be part of Cuban and American sport history. She was proud to have been part of the reconnection of the AAGPBL players, and she was very proud that the "stuff [I] saved would be seen by the girls." As her friend and biographer, I think Lefty would be proud of something else she has helped to create.

In 2013 five former players from the AAGPBL—Maybelle Blair, Shirley Burkovich, Karen Kunkel, Jane Moffet, and Mary Moore—working with me and Donna Cohen, created the International Women's Baseball Center (IWBC). At our first meeting we talked about the importance of preserving the players' history, as well as about bringing the larger story of women's baseball to the fore. As some of those same women had done years before when they created the AAGPBL Players' Association, the IWBC used the threads of friendship, teamwork, and baseball to create a group dedicated to preserving the long and expansive history of women's baseball. The IWBC chose the word "center" to describe the organization and facility we are building because it will be more than a museum. It will preserve and house collections from women's baseball worldwide, but it will also use that history to educate, inspire, and promote equal access for girls and women. Lefty was not at that first meeting of the IWBC, but she consistently supported our efforts. She told me, "I am happy you are building this for us, for all us girls." Calling it "Blair's Museum" because she knew that Maybelle Blair was the driving force behind the center, Lefty understood how important it was to tell and preserve their history. She was excited to have her memorabilia and her story represented in the IWBC. Only a portion of Lefty's collection will be housed there, but because of her foresight, a younger generation of girls and women will be able to see and touch part of their own history.

Lefty's collection, when made publicly available, will help to make it harder for people to deny that women's baseball has a past. After those years when no one wanted to hear that she had played professional baseball, Lefty understood the devastation of that erasure of history. For too long the history of women's baseball has been ignored, but collections such as this one, combined with the written and spoken stories about women's role in baseball, make it harder to deny that history. It is crucial for growth to know that we stand on the shoulders of others, and a large part of Lefty's legacy is that through her "gift to them" more girls will benefit from that knowledge.

"Legacy" is not a word Lefty would ever use in relation to herself. She consistently resisted the suggestion that she was special or a role model. She never openly bragged about her life as either a baseball player or her experience as a brave and solitary fifteen-year-old immigrant. She repeatedly points out that she was not a superstar. She did not get a college degree or move up the ladder at her job; instead she was, in her words, "pretty boring and not very successful, just common." I would argue against that characterization. Her determination to survive and find a way despite heavy odds against her and the way she was able to find strength through her love of sport make her a hero. But at the same time I would argue that what she called her "commonness" may just be her most important legacy. We are used to hearing about the best baseball players, the ones who became all-stars or who went on to greatness in other fields. It has traditionally been common to tell the stories of the winners. It is as if stories like Lefty's, stories that either did not champion or expand the traditional narrative of the American success story, are simply not worth telling. Few of us will ever be all-stars or make the kind of mark in the world that usually warrants fame. But we seek role models for our lives and are usually drawn to those who are most like us. For immigrants and for girls who love sports, where do we turn? How do we survive daily struggles at our job, carve out a place for our daughters to play baseball, or recreate ourselves when life changes so drastically that we can, like Lefty, literally no longer order food at a restaurant? Lefty's legacy is clear to those of us who seek it out. It is one of diversity, strength, courage, and the ability to look forward. It is a legacy that crosses cultural and geographic boundaries and provides a model of how some women use sport to overcome life's challenges.

Without sport Lefty would have never survived the difficulties of school, a troubled family, and the ever-changing expectations of her mother. It provided her with a retreat, a place where she was safe, and, most important, a place where she believed herself to be good. Sport gave her the confidence to pack a suitcase and fly to America at age fifteen. The physical and emotional memory of how it felt to be good on the ball field provided her with the strength to persevere in those days after the league ended and she started to drink heavily. Finally, the development of the AAGPBL Players' Association and the reconnection with those players continued to provide Lefty with the family and support she required to live into old age. "Was sports important?" Lefty asks in bafflement at the question. "Is it more a part of me than anything else? Well, holy cow! What do you think?" For women like Lefty, sport is not just a concept; it is part of their physical, emotional, and cultural makeup. Without sport Lefty's life would have been far scarier, a lot less fulfilled, and "overwhelmingly empty."

Lefty's life exemplifies what I call sport-identity. Sport-identity is a category that works very much like race, class, gender, and sexuality do in defining and shaping identity. Like traditional categories, sport-identity can be used to expand the many intersections and layers that make up identity. For example, we could certainly write Lefty's story through the traditional lenses of gender, race, and class, but what we would miss is what *she* believes is the most important part of her: her sport-identity. Lefty sums up: "It was my life in sports, my connections to sports that saved me. Holy cow! Where would I have been? Where would I be without it?" Lefty is a particularly good example of sport-identity. She rarely identifies herself as only Cuban, only working class, or only a woman. Instead she nearly always refers to herself as a female Cuban American baseball player. For women like Lefty, sport is the location where all other identity markers merge to create self-expression and self-awareness. We cannot understand her if we don't use sport, and she most certainly would not recognize herself if sport were not part of the equation.

In recent years Lefty's dementia has deepened. She has become more isolated and is rarely able to attend AAGPBL events. Before 2016 I had not seen Lefty for a few years. Over Labor Day weekend that year, the IWBC held a dedication ceremony on its new property, located across the street from Beyer Stadium, the home of the Rockford Peaches. The date of the dedication was purposely chosen to coincide with the Peach Orchard Classic, an annual women's baseball tournament held every year at Beyer. Hundreds of people, local dignitaries, television crews, and even a reporter from Sweden were there.

The IWBC founders, Rockford city leaders, and actresses from *A League of Their Own* were all seated on the stage as the dedication began. I sat listening to the usual thanks and introductions, nervously waiting for my turn to speak, when I saw out of the corner of my eye a young woman leading an older woman to the front row. As I rose to speak, I found myself looking into the eyes of Lefty Alvarez. Given the distance from the stage, I was pretty sure she did not recognize me. But I was nervous anyway, and it took me a minute to recover. Once I did, though, I gave perhaps the most important speech of my life. When it was over, there was no way to tell what Lefty thought or even if any of it registered with her. I got my answer later that day when she held my face in her hands and said, "I am proud." It is we who should be proud to learn from and stand on the shoulders of Lefty Alvarez.

In the face of dementia and the physical challenges of aging, Lefty's definition of being a rascal has changed. But whether it is the feeling of success when she is able to recognize an old friend or the triumph at some other daily activity such as walking without a cane, Lefty still relies on her "sport self" for solace and comfort. On the days when she is confused and mobility is difficult, Lefty needs that part of herself the most. The night after the IWBC dedication ceremony at a restaurant where the after-dedication ceremonies continued, Lefty was helped in by an aide. She sat in a corner, and as was often the case, people began flooding in to see her. After about an hour of this attention Lefty grabbed her cane and struggled to her feet. Several of us noticed and attempted to help. She waved us off, stood upright, and, with a look I have come to realize means "Take that!," she nodded and headed out the door. In what was obviously not a conscious effort to draw on her sport-identity, she did just that. Lefty gathered the strength to stand tall, and with confidence she walked out of the room. She was mentally determined and even physically strong in that moment. She was the rascal of El Cerro one more time.

APPENDIX I

LEFTY ALVAREZ BASEBALL STATISTICS

SEASONAL PITCHING RECORDS

YEAR	G	IP	R	ER	ERA	BB	SO	HB	WP	W	L	PCT
1950	12	—	—	—	—	—	—	—	—	6	6	.500
1951	13	34	29	14	3.71	26	7	2	2	2	0	1.000

SEASONAL BATTING RECORDS

YEAR	G	AB	R	H	2B	3B	HR	RBI	SB	BB	SO	AVG
1949	—	—	—	—	—	—	—	—	—	—	—	—
1950	12	39	4	10	0	1	0	3	0	4	3	.256
1951	17	21	1	2	1	0	0	1	0	1	2	.095
1953	53	123	4	24	4	0	0	12	0	7	9	.195
1954	23	68	6	13	2	0	0	2	3	2	5	.191

Information gathered from https://www.aagpbl.org/profiles/isabel-alvarez-lefty/276. Accessed March 28, 2019.

1866 First organized women's baseball teams in United States are started at Vassar College.

1867 The Dolly Vardens of Philadelphia become the first professional black women's team.

1875 The first women's baseball game for which fans were charged and players were paid is played between the Blondes and the Brunettes in Springfield, Illinois, on September 11.

1876 The Resolutes, modeled after the Vassar College team, develop their own version of uniforms, which included long-sleeved shirts with frilled high necklines; embroidered belts; wide, floor-length skirts; high-button shoes; and broad striped caps.

1880 A Smith College baseball team is disbanded after disapproving mothers complain about their children playing the sport, saying it is not appropriate for women to play.

1898 Lizzie Arlington becomes the first woman to sign a professional baseball contract; she signed with the Philadelphia Reserves.

1890s-1935 Women's "Bloomer Girls" clubs barnstorm across the United States and play men's town, semipro, and Minor League teams; Bloomer teams had an average of three males on them; Rogers Hornsby and Smokey Joe Wood, dressed as women, got their starts with Bloomer Girls teams.

1900s Bloomer Girls introduce night baseball games.

1904 Amanda Clement is the first woman to be paid to umpire a baseball game; she umpired professionally for six years after that.

1908 Maud Nelson is the starting pitcher for the men's Cherokee Indian Base Ball Club.

1908   The U.S. baseball national anthem, "Take Me Out to the Ball Game," is inspired by and written about a young girl's love of the game.

1911-16   The St. Louis Cardinals are owned by Helene Britton.

1920s   Philadelphia has factory teams for women, women's leagues, and the Philadelphia Bobbies for nonworking women.

1920s   Mary O'Gara takes the Philadelphia Bobbies to Japan to play men's teams.

1928   Lizzie Murphy becomes the first woman to play for a Major League team in an exhibition game; she also became the first person of either gender to play for both the American League and National League in All-Star games.

1928   Mary Gisolo joins the nationwide American Legion Junior Baseball Program and helps to lead the Blanford Cubs to the Indiana state title.

1931   Jackie Mitchell strikes out Babe Ruth and Lou Gehrig, back to back, in an exhibition game against the New York Yankees while playing for the AA Chattanooga Lookouts.

1930s   The "Bold Years" for women's baseball; women baseball players tour internationally, play junior baseball, and sign Minor League contracts.

1934   Olympic hero Babe Didrikson pitches exhibition games for the Athletics, Cardinals, and Indians.

1943-54   The AAGPBL is started by Philip Wrigley, owner of the Chicago Cubs and Wrigley's Chewing Gum.

1944   Dottie Wiltse pitches for the AAGPBL up until she is six months pregnant.

1946   Edith Houghton becomes the first woman to scout for the Major Leagues.

1946   Sophie Kurys sets the single-season stolen base record for the AAGPBL with 201 steals in 203 attempts; this record continues to be unequaled in baseball history, as Ricky Henderson is second in stolen bases with 130 (set in 1982).

1947   The Racine Belles of the AAGPBL start the Junior Belles baseball program; one hundred girls try out, and sixty are selected to play on four teams: the Grays, Greens, Reds, and Golds.

1947   Eulalia Gonzales becomes the first Cuban woman to play baseball in the United States; she played with the Racine Belles.

1948   The Junior Belles become more popular as more girls try out for the teams; other AAGPBL teams, such as the Lassies and the Comets, begin to sponsor girls' junior baseball teams.

1948   After five years of playing, players in the AAGPBL start throwing pitches overhand instead of underhand.

1950   The Racine Belles and Junior Belles fold due to lack of money.

1950s   Toni Stone, Connie Morgan, and Mamie "Peanut" Johnson play on men's professional teams in the Negro Leagues; they aren't allowed to play in the AAGPBL because they are African Americans.

1952   George Trautman voids Eleanor Engle's Minor League contract with the AA Harrisburg Senators.

1952   On June 23 organized baseball bans women from the Minor Leagues; the ban remains in effect today.

1955   Bill Allington forms two women's teams, called the Allington's All-Stars, which barnstorm across the United States playing men's town and semipro teams, as the Bloomer Girls did; the teams last until 1957.

1969   Bernice Gera becomes the first woman to sign a professional umpire contract.

1971   Gloria Jean "Jackie" Jackson tries out for the Pittsfield Senators; she receives an offer from the Raleigh Durham Triangles, but the offer is revoked one day later.

1973   The Pawtucket Slaterettes become the first all-girls' baseball league.

1974   Girls win the right to play baseball in Little League baseball through Title IX.

1976   Christine Wren umpires in Class A Northwest League (Minor Leagues).

1977-78 Pam Postema umpires, with high marks, in the Rookie Gulf Coast League.

1979-80 Pam Postema umpires in Class A Florida State League.

1981-82 Pam Postema umpires in Class AA Texas League.

1983 Pam Postema moves up to Triple A Pacific Coast League.

1984 Bob Hope founds the Sun Sox, a Class A Minor League all-women's team; he tries to enter the team into the Class A Florida State League; the league doesn't award Hope the franchise because of male chauvinism; Henry "Hank" Aaron is the team's director of player personnel.

1988 Pam Postema is invited by baseball commissioner Bart Giamatti to umpire spring training games and the Hall of Fame game.

1988 The American Women's Baseball Association (AWBA) is founded in Chicago; It is the first organized women's league since the AAGPBL; six players from the AWBA are extras in the movie *A League of Their Own*.

1988 Julie Croteau plays semipro baseball for the Fredericksburg Giants of the Virginia Baseball League.

1989 Pam Postema is again invited by baseball commissioner Bart Giamatti to umpire spring training games.

1989 Bart Giamatti dies; as a result, Pam Postema is released from umpiring in the Minor Leagues, ending her dream of umpiring in the Major Leagues; she umpired for thirteen years in the Minors.

1989 Julie Croteau becomes the first woman to play collegiate men's varsity baseball; she does so at St. Mary's College (NCAA Division III).

1990s The American Women's Baseball League (AWBL; also known as American Women's Baseball, AWB) is founded by Jim Glennie in an effort to unite women's baseball teams and leagues around the country and to provide them support.

1992 *A League of Their Own*, about the AAGPBL, is produced by Penny Marshall.

1993 Sal Coats becomes the first woman to play in the Men's Senior Baseball League (MSBL) World Series.

1994 Julie Croteau and Lee Anne Ketcham (Beanie Ketcham) (Colorado Silver Bullets players) join the Maui Stingrays of the Hawaiian Winter Baseball League, becoming the first women to play in a Major League Baseball (MLB)-sanctioned league.

1994 Bob Hope forms and the Coors Brewing Company sponsors the Colorado Silver Bullets women's baseball team, which plays men's college and Minor League teams; the team existed for four years.

1994 The Women's National Adult Baseball Association (WNABA) is formed; sixteen women's teams play in a women's world series in Phoenix.

1995 The WNABA has one hundred affiliated women's baseball teams in sixteen states in the United States.

1995 Ila Borders becomes the first woman to pitch and win a complete collegiate baseball game; Ila also is the first woman to win a collegiate baseball scholarship.

1995 Julie Croteau becomes the first woman to coach baseball in a men's NCAA Division I baseball program; she is the assistant coach at the University of Massachusetts–Amherst in 1995–1996.

1998 Ila Borders becomes the first woman to win a men's pro game while pitching for the Duluth Dukes, an independent Minor League team.

1997 Ladies League Baseball is formed by Mike Ribant, a San Diego businessman; it becomes the first professional women's baseball league since the AAGPBL; the San Jose Spitfires win the championship this year over the Los Angeles Legends.

1998 After beginning its second season, Ladies League Baseball expands to six teams and goes nationwide but folds shortly after due to a lack of attendance.

2000 The AWBL takes a women's baseball team to Japan to play Team Energen, the Japanese women's national team.

2001 The first Women's World Series (WWS) is played at the Sky-Dome in Toronto, Ontario, Canada; the United States, Australia,

Canada, and Japan participate; the United States wins the gold medal.

2003   The Pawtucket Slaterettes all-girls' baseball league celebrates its thirtieth season of all-girls' baseball.

2003   Women's baseball becomes an official sport (the thirty-ninth) of the AAU; this marks the first time in U.S. history that a U.S. national organization begins sanctioning and supporting women's baseball.

2003   The American Eagles of the American Women's Baseball Federation (AWBF) becomes the first women's baseball team to be sanctioned by USA Baseball.

2004   The first-ever Women's Baseball World Cup is played in Edmonton, Alberta, Canada, July 30–August 8; the event is sanctioned by the International Baseball Association and Federation (IBAF) and is hosted by Baseball Canada.

2004   USA Baseball sanctions the first official national women's baseball team; the team competes in the 2004 WWS (in Japan) and in the 2004 Women's World Cup of Baseball.

2004   John Kovach, manager of the South Bend Blue Sox Women's Baseball Club, director of the Great Lakes Women's Baseball League, and AAU Women's Baseball Youth Baseball chair, works out a proposal with Little League, Inc. to use the Michiana Girls' Baseball League (a league that Kovach founded in 2002) as a model league to develop girls' Little League baseball programs around the country; Little League started as a boys' softball program in 2000 because five hundred boys were playing in Little League softball leagues around the United States, but the organization failed to start a girls' baseball program, although thousands of girls were also playing baseball in Little League baseball leagues around the country.

2007   The Chicago Pioneers girls' baseball team becomes the first-ever U.S. Girls' Baseball National Champions after defeating the Pawtucket Slaterettes during the 2007 Women's Baseball

National Championship/Girls' Baseball National Championship in Ft. Myers, Florida.

2008 Eri Yoshida, sixteen, becomes Japan's first professional female baseball player to play in a men's league by signing a professional contract with the Kobe 9 Cruise of a new Japanese independent league. Japan once had a female professional baseball federation in the 1950s.

2010 Tiffany Brooks becomes the first woman in the United States to sign a pro baseball contract in the twenty-first century; she signs with the Big Bend Cowboys of the independent Continental Baseball League.

2010s Ghazaleh Sailors and Marti Sementelli sign on to play college ball.

Sailors moves from Santa Barbara, California, to play baseball at the University of Maine–Presque Isle. She is among only a handful of women who have earned an NCAA baseball victory on the mound. Sailors pitches five innings of six-hit ball in a 13–1, five-inning win over NCAA Division III provisional member Valley Forge Christian College at Phoenixville, Pennsylvania.

Sementelli played Little League Baseball in Sherman Oaks, California. During high school she spent two years on the baseball team at Burbank High and two years playing for Matt Mowry at Birmingham High. While at Birmingham, she pitched a complete game against San Marcos High School of Santa Barbara, throwing 102 pitches. At fifteen, she competed with Team USA at the Women's World Cup of Baseball. In 2011 she earned a baseball scholarship to Montreat College in North Carolina.

2011 The first-ever member clubs are announced for Southern Ontario's Women's Baseball League. Those clubs are located in London, Guelph, St. Catharines, and Niagara Falls, Ontario, Canada. This is the first-ever professional league for women (aged eighteen and over) in Ontario; it starts playing in 2012.

2014 Mone Davis pitches in the Little League World Series (LLWS). She is one of two girls who plays in the series and is the first girl to earn a win and to pitch a shutout in the series' history. She is the eighteenth girl overall to play, the sixth to get a hit, and the first African American. She is also the first Little League baseball player to appear on the cover of *Sports Illustrated*.

2014   Over pizza and beer Maybelle Blair, Shirley Burkovich, Kat Williams, Donna Cohen, Jane Moffett, and Karen Kunkel create the International Women's Baseball Center (IWBC). In 2016 J&M Plating donates two buildings and property located across the street from Beyer Stadium in Rockford, Illinois, for the center.

2015   The Red Sox hold first all-female fantasy baseball camp.

2015   Women's baseball is added to the 2015 Pan American Games.

2016   Twelve teams compete in the seventh Women's Baseball World Cup—the most in history.

2016   Jessica Mendoza is hired by ESPN to call baseball games.

2016   The Seattle Mariners hire Amanda Hopkins as a full-time amateur scout, making her the first female to hold that position in MLB in almost sixty years.

Robin Wallace is hired by MLB Scouting Bureau. She had been an assistant general manager and general manager for independent Minor League baseball teams, was the only female on a ten-person U.S. coaching staff for the World Children's Baseball Fair in Japan in 2010, and coached an all-girls' team in a Baseball for All tournament in Cooperstown, New York. She was inducted into the National Women's Baseball Hall of Fame in 2002 and from 2003 until 2009 she served as executive director of the North American Women's Baseball League.

2017   Claire Smith wins J. G. Taylor Spink Award. She covered the New York Yankees from 1983 to 1987 as the first female MLB beat writer, working for the *Hartford Courant*. She later worked as a columnist for the *New York Times* from 1991 to 1998 and was an editor and columnist for the *Philadelphia Inquirer* from 1998 to 2007. She was also a news editor for ESPN.

Smith was elected the 2017 recipient of the J. G. Taylor Spink Award in balloting by the Baseball Writers' Association of America (BBWAA) on December 6, 2016. She is the first woman and fourth African American to receive this award, the BBWAA's highest honor, presented annually since 1962 for "meritorious contributions to baseball writing." The award is permanently on view in the Scribes and Mikemen exhibit in the library of the National Baseball Hall of Fame and Museum in Cooperstown.

2017   The Trailblazers series—approximately one hundred girls, ages sixteen and under, representing twenty states, the District of Columbia, and Canada—begins play in the first-of-its-kind tournament starting April 13. The tournament concludes on April 15, seventy years to the day when Dodger legend Jackie Robinson broke the color barrier in the Major Leagues.

2017   Emma Charlesworth-Seiler and Jen Pawol umpire in the Minor Leagues. For just the second time in Minor League history, two women umpire in affiliated leagues at the same time. The first time was in 2004. Charlesworth-Seiler's and Pawol's simultaneous work represents progress in a sport where women have been opposed and often harassed for trying to officiate since Bernice Gera, the first female umpire in professional baseball, sued to work in the New York–Penn League in 1972.

Information gathered from https://www.usabaseball.com /about/history/, accessed March 28, 2019.

NOTES

INTRODUCTION

1. At the second AAGPBL I attended in 2004, Lefty proclaimed that since she and Jane Moffet now knew me, I could be her "carrier of things."
2. Pettavino and Pye, *Sport in Cuba*, 25.
3. Cahn, *Coming on Strong*, introduction.

1. EL CERRO

1. Vilaboy, *Cuba*, 14–15.
2. Vilaboy, *Cuba*, 14.
3. Vilaboy, *Cuba*, 21.
4. Vilaboy, *Cuba*, 22–23.
5. Clodfelter, *Warfare and Armed Conflicts*, 306.
6. Vilaboy, *Cuba*, 24.
7. Vilaboy, *Cuba*, 25.
8. Vilaboy, *Cuba*, 26.
9. David Gimenez, "The Little War or Guerra Chiquita," Cuba Heritage.org, accessed January 13, 2018, http://www.cubaheritage.org/articles.asp?lID=1&artID=148.
10. Gimenez, "The Little War or Guerra Chiquita."
11. Gimenez, "The Little War or Guerra Chiquita."
12. Navarro, *History of Cuba*, 55–57.
13. Quoted in Lehman, *Colonialism to Independence*, 114.
14. Martí, *José Martí Reader*, 190–200.
15. Jerry A. Sierra, "The War for Cuban Independence," History of Cuba.org, accessed January 13, 2018, http://www.historyofcuba.com/history/scaw/scaw1a.htm.
16. Sierra, "The War for Cuban Independence."
17. Sierra, "The War for Cuban Independence."
18. Sierra, "The War for Cuban Independence."
19. Quoted in Campbell. "Not Likely Sent."
20. Navarro, *History of Cuba*, 71.
21. Navarro, *History of Cuba*, 70–73.
22. Navarro, *History of Cuba*, 70–74.

23. The Platt Amendment was a rider attached to the U.S. Army appropriations bill of March 1901, stipulating the conditions for withdrawal of U.S. troops remaining in Cuba since the Spanish-American War and molding fundamental Cuban-U.S. relations until 1934.

24. Perez, *Cuba: Between Reform and Revolution*, 196.

25. Perez, *Cuba: Between Reform and Revolution*, 190.

26. Perez, *Cuba: Between Reform and Revolution*, 190–91.

27. Quoted in Langley, *The Banana Wars*, 13–14.

28. Perez, *Cuba: Between Reform and Revolution*, 206.

29. Perez, *Cuba: Between Reform and Revolution*, 214.

30. Perez, *Cuba: Between Reform and Revolution*, 217.

31. Perez, *Cuba: Between Reform and Revolution*, 253–55.

32. The Hawley-Smoot Tariff implemented protectionist trade policies sponsored by Senator Reed Smoot and Representative Willis C. Hawley; it was signed into law on June 17, 1930.

33. Ewell, *The Human Tradition in Latin America*, 79–80.

34. Perez, *Cuba: Between Reform and Revolution*, 255–60.

35. Thomas, *Cuba*, 607–9.

36. Thomas, *Cuba*, 610.

37. Perez, *Cuba: Between Reform and Revolution*, 261.

38. Perez, *Cuba: Between Reform and Revolution*, 265.

39. Thomas, *Cuba*, 637–38.

40. http://www.examiner.com/article/my-surname-is-valdes-havana-s-casa-de-beneficencia-orphanage. Accessed January 30, 2017.

41. http://www.examiner.com/article/my-surname-is-valdes-havana-s-casa-de-beneficencia-orphanage. Accessed January 30, 2017.

42. Melena del Sur is located south of Mayabeque Province in Cuba. There are several versions regarding the meaning of the name "Melena." The region is home to some Greeks (*melanie* means "black" in Greek); black was the predominant color of some of the region's most fertile land. Many still debate whether it was on its shores or in neighboring Batabanó that the city of Havana was founded in 1515. Because Havana was possibly founded in Melena del Sur, the region's coat of arms is the Latin phrase "Havana primo hic est condit."

2. REFASHIONING LEFTY

1. Stoner, *From the House to the Streets*, Kindle locations 1043–47.

2. Stoner, *From the House to the Streets*, Kindle locations 1043–47.

3. Perez, *Cuba: Between Reform and Revolution*, 241.

4. Stoner, *From the House to the Streets*, Kindle locations 1043–47.

5. Perez, *Cuba: Between Reform and Revolution*, 241.

6. Pettavino and Pye, *Sport in Cuba*, 22.

7. Pettavino and Pye, *Sport in Cuba*, 50–51.

8. Pettavino and Pye, *Sport in Cuba*, 24.

9. Quoted in Pettavino and Pye, *Sport in Cuba*, 24.

10. Quoted in Isabel Alvarez, "Alvarez, Isabel 'Lefty' (Interview transcript and video), 2009," *Digital Collections*, accessed June 2017, https://digitalcollections.library.gvsu.edu/document/29660.

11. Pettavino and Pye, *Sport in Cuba*, 51–52.

12. Pettavino and Pye, *Sport in Cuba*, 51–52.

3. THE PASSION OF THE ISLAND

1. Pettavino and Pye, *Sport in Cuba*, 25.

2. Echevarría, *The Pride of Havana*, 90.

3. Echevarría, *The Pride of Havana*, 90.

4. Pettavino and Pye, *Sport in Cuba*, 26–27.

5. Pettavino and Pye, *Sport in Cuba*, 27.

6. Pettavino and Pye, *Sport in Cuba*, 27.

7. Echevarría, *The Pride of Havana*, 112–15.

8. Pettavino and Pye, *Sport in Cuba*, 27

9. Pettavino and Pye, *Sport in Cuba*, 27.

10. Echevarría, *The Pride of Havana*, 15.

11. Fidler, *Origins and History*, 99.

12. AAGPBL, news release, September 12, 1947, Meyerhoff Files, Drawer 75, 1947 News Release Folder, All-American Girls Professional Baseball League Collection, Northern Indiana Center for History, South Bend, Indiana.

13. Quoted in "History of the League during 1947 and 1948," Dailey records, 1943–1946; Joyce Sports Research Collection, University of Notre Dame Library, Special Collection, South Bend, Indiana.

14. Kamenshek's statistics are well known and can be found on the league's website, aagpbl.org. Kurys remains one of the all-time great base stealers in baseball. Her cleats are alongside those of Ricky Henderson in the Baseball Hall of Fame in Cooperstown, New York.

15. Fidler, *Origins and History*, 111.

16. Fidler, *Origins and History*, 88.

17. Press release from AAGPBL, April 12, 1948; Northern Indiana Historical Association.

18. Quoted in Fidler, *Origins and History*, 111.

19. Fidler, *Origins and History*, 111.

20. Fidler, *Origins and History*, 111–112.

21. Copy of South American tour schedule, August 15, 1947; Meyerhoff Files, Drawer 74, SA Tour Folder, All-American Girls Professional Baseball League Collection, Northern Indiana Center for History, South Bend, Indiana. Also housed in Northern Indiana Center for History, South Bend, Indiana.

22. Copy of South American tour schedule, August 15, 1947; Meyerhoff Files, Drawer 74, SA Tour Folder, All-American Girls Professional Baseball League Collection, Northern Indiana Center for History, South Bend, Indiana.

23. Max Carey to tour players, October 23, 1947; Meyerhoff Files, Drawer 74, SA Tour Folder, All-American Girls Professional Baseball League Collection, Northern Indiana Center for History, South Bend, Indiana.

24. Mary Rountree to Max Carey, January 31, 1948; Meyerhoff Files, Drawer 74, SA Tour Folder, All-American Girls Professional Baseball League Collection, Northern Indiana Center for History, South Bend, Indiana.

25. AAGPBL news release, February 10, 1949; Meyerhoff Files, Drawer 74, 1949 Tour Publicity Folder, All-American Girls Professional Baseball League Collection, Northern Indiana Center for History, South Bend, Indiana.

26. Fidler, *Origins and History*, 115.

27. Max Carey to tour players, October 23, 1947; Meyerhoff Files, Drawer 74, SA Tour Folder, All-American Girls Professional Baseball League Collection, Northern Indiana Center for History, South Bend, Indiana.

28. Cuadras, *El Nicaragüense*, 241–42. In an essay Cuadras suggests that the baseball player has a certain Odyssean quality—"leaving home, traveling around the world filled with countless difficulties, and then returning"—and this sort of journey fits with the Nicaraguan's potential for creative imagination (Cuadras in Arellano, *El béisbol en Nicaragua*, 13–14).

29. Cuadras discussed in Purdy, "Revolutionary Béisbol," 6.

30. Cuadras quoted in Purdy, "Revolutionary Béisbol," 6.

31. See also Fidler, *Origins and History*, 119.

32. "Empatada ayer la serie de base-ball femenino," *La Nueva Prensa* (Managua), February 4, 1949.

33. Press release from AAGPBL, February 10, 1949; Northern Indiana Historical Association.

34. Ruth Richard diary entries, reprinted in Fidler, *Origins and History*, 117.

35. Ruth Richard diary, February 10–12, 1949. Reprinted in Fidler, *Origins and History*, 220.

36. Ruth Richard diary, February 10–12, 1949. Reprinted in Fidler, *Origins and History*, 220.

4. COMING TO AMERICA

1. Perry R. Duis, "World War II," The Encyclopedia of Chicago, accessed March 3, 2019, http://www.encyclopedia.chicagohistory.org/pages/1384.html.
2. U.S. Census Bureau, "Illinois: Number of Inhabitants," accessed April 2019, https://www2.census.gov/library/publications/decennial/1950/population -volume-1/vol-01-16.pdf.
3. Emalee Nelson, "Cuban Babe (Ruth): The Story of Seven Cubana Women in Professional Baseball," Sport in American History, October 17, 2016, https:// ussporthistory.com/2016/10/17/cuban-babe-ruth-the-story-of-seven-cubana -women-in-professional-baseball/.
4. Mary Louise Baumgartner, "Baumgartner, Mary Louise "Wimp (Interview transcript and video), 2010," Digital Collections, accessed January 2018, https:// digitalcollections.library.gvsu.edu/document/29692.
5. See also Fidler, *Origins and History*, 92.
6. See also Fidler, *Origins and History*, 92.
7. See also Fidler, *Origins and History*, 92.
8. "Isabel Alvarez," All-American Girls Professional Baseball League, accessed March 4, 2019, http://www.aagpbl.org/profiles/isabel-alvarez-lefty/276.
9. See also Fidler, *Origins and History*, 92.
10. See also Fidler, *Origins and History*, 92.
11. See also Fidler, *Origins and History*, 92.
12. See also Fidler, *Origins and History*, 92.
13. See also Fidler, *Origins and History*, 92.
14. AAGPBL news release, August 22, 1950, Dailey records, 195.
15. Fidler, *Origins and History*, 111.
16. Fidler, *Origins and History*, 137.
17. "Isabel Alvarez," All-American Girls Professional Baseball League, accessed March 2019, http://www.aagpbl.org/profiles/isabel-alvarez-lefty/276.
18. Fidler, *Origins and History*, 203.
19. Fidler, *Origins and History*, 137; Harold Dailey papers, Notre Dame Archives, vol. 6, October 31,1951, and vol. 7, August 15, 1952.
20. Harold Dailey papers, Notre Dame Archives, vol. 6, October 31, 1951, and vol. 7, August 15, 1952.
21. Harold Dailey papers, Notre Dame Archives, vol. 8, December 1, 1952–September 30, 1953.

22. Harold Dailey papers, Notre Dame Archives, vol. 8, December 1, 1952–September 30, 1953.

23. Official website of the AAGPBL, aagpbl.org/index.cfm. Accessed March 2019.

24. Official website of the AAGPBL, aagpbl.org/index.cfm.

25. Bob Renner, "Sports Onceover," *News-Sentinel* (Fort Wayne IN), September 16, 1953; Notre Dame Archives.

26. Fidler, *Origins and History*, 135–37.

27. Joe Doyle, "According to Doyle . . . ," *South Bend Tribune*, February 12, 1954; Notre Dame Archives.

28. "Girls League Votes to Suspend Play," *South Bend Tribune*, January 25, 1954; Earle MacCammon to Directors, February 22, 1954; Notre Dame Archives.

29. Fidler, *Origins and History*, 133–38.

30. *Daisy Fan News*, April 30, 1954, International Women's Baseball Center (IWBC) Archives. www.internationalwomensbaseballcenter.org.

31. *Daisy Fan News*, April 30, 1954, IWBC Archives

31. *Daisy Fan News*, April 30, 1954, IWBC Archives.

33. *Daisy Fan News*, 30 April 40, 1954, IWBC Archives.

34. Meeting minutes, September 17, 1954, Notre Dame Archives.

35. *Kalamazoo (MI) Gazette*, January 31, 1955, 33; Notre Dame Archives.

36. "American Girls Baseball League Votes One-Year Suspension," *Kalamazoo (MI) Gazette*, January 31, 1955, 16; Notre Dame Archives.

5. LIFE AFTER THE LEAGUE

1. Quoted in Sargent, *We Were the All-Americans*, 123.

2. Berlage, *Women in Baseball*, 134.

3. Perez, *Cuba: Between Reform and Revolution*, 288–92.

4. Caryn E. Neumann, "Cuban immigrants," Immigration to the United States, accessed July 2017, http://immigrationtounitedstates.org/453-cuban-immigrants .html.

5. Neumann, "Cuban immigrants."

6. Neumann, "Cuban immigrants."

7. Perez, *Cuba: Between Reform and Revolution*, 331.

8. Perez, *Cuba: Between Reform and Revolution*, 332.

9. Quoted in Doran, *A Road Well Traveled*, 20.

10. Al Hart, "Women's History: How Young Women Shook Up GE in the '70s," UE News, February 27, 2015, http://www.ueunion.org/ue-news/2015/womens -history-how-young-women-shook-up-ge-in-the-70s.

11. Hart, "Women's History."

12. Hart, "Women's History."

13. "Good Medicine for Cuba," *New York Times*, March 8, 1978, http://www.nytimes
.com/1978/03/08/archives/good-medicine-for-cuba.html?_r=0.

14. David Binder, "U.S. and Cuba Prepare to Draft a Maritime Agreement," *New
York Times*, January 15, 1978, http://www.nytimes.com/1978/01/15/archives/us
-and-cuba-prepare-to-draft-a-maritime-agreement-a-twoyear-period.html.

15. Teddy Kapur and Alastair Smith, "Housing Policy in Castro's Cuba," May 16,
2002, http://www.housingfinance.org/uploads/Publicationsmanager/Caribbean
_Cuba_HousinginCastrosCuba.pdf.

6. A LEAGUE OF HER OWN

1. Quoted in Fidler, *Origins and History*, 229.

2. Fidler, *Origins and History*, 229.

3. Fidler, *Origins and History*, 229.

4. This was a three-day event for women in athletic competition that grew into an
eleven-day, nineteen-sport festival attracting three thousand participants to
Fort Wayne each September. Run, Jane, Run, Inc. was established in 1986 as a
separate not-for-profit agency. Over the next twenty years Run, Jane, Run grew
into one of the largest amateur multi-sport events for women in the nation, with
franchises run by not-for-profit organizations in South Bend, Grand Rapids,
Louisville, Cleveland, Pittsburgh, Salt Lake City, Phoenix, Tulsa, and Engle-
wood, New Jersey. Women's Bureau, http://womensbureau.org/who-we-are
/history-highlights.

5. *Today's News*, AAGPBL newsletter, October 1981.

6. Quoted in Fidler, *Origins and History*, 236.

7. Quoted in *Today's News*, AAGPBL newsletter, August 1982.

8. Fidler, *Origins and History*, 238.

9. *Today's News*, AAGPBL newsletter August 1982.

10. Quoted in Fidler, *Origins and History*, 279.

11. Perez, *Cuba: Between Reform and Revolution*, 382–87

12. Perez, *Cuba: Between Reform and Revolution*, 382–84

13. Fidler, *The Origins and History*, 243.

14. From the AAGPBL newsletter *Extra Innings* (April 1986); author's personal
collection.

15. Quoted in Fidler, *Origins and History*, 253–55.

16. Quoted in Fidler, *Origins and History*, 280.

17. Quoted in *News Sentinel* (Fort Wayne), July 23, 2008.

18. Quoted in Terry Donahue, "Donahue, Terry (Interview transcript and video), 2010," *Digital Collections*, accessed January 2017, https://digitalcollections.library .gvsu.edu/document/29693.

19. Terry Doran, *Latin Nights: The Baseball Journey of Isabel Alvarez*, Internet Archive, accessed March 2018 https://archive.org/details/LatinNightsThe BaseballJourneyOfIsabelAlvarez.

EPILOGUE

1. Alvarez collection. Publicity poster for game in Puerto Rico, 1949.

2. "AAGPBL," *The Canadian Baseball Hall of Fame and Museum* (blog), accessed March 2017, http://baseballhalloffame.ca/inductees/aagbpl.

BIBLIOGRAPHY

All-American Girls Professional Baseball League Collection. Baseball Hall of Fame Research Library, Cooperstown, New York.

Ardell, Jean. *Breaking into Baseball: Women and the National Past Time.* Carbondale: Southern Illinois Press, 2005.

Arellano, Jorge Eduardo, ed. *El béisbol en Nicaragua: Rescate histórico y cultural, 1889-1948.* Managua: Academia de Geografía e Historia de Nicaragua, 2007.

Barnes, Mark. *The Spanish-American War and Philippine Insurrection, 1898-1902.* New York: Routledge, 2010.

Berlage, Gai. *Women in Baseball: The Forgotten History.* Westport CT: Praeger, 1994.

Brown, Patricia. *A League of My Own: Memoirs of a Pitcher for the All-American Girls Professional Baseball League.* Jefferson NC: McFarland, 2003.

Browne, Lois. *The Girls of Summer: The Real Story of the All-American Girls Professional Baseball League.* New York: HarperCollins, 1992.

Bullock, Steven R. *Playing for Their Nation: Baseball and the American Military during World War II.* Lincoln: University of Nebraska Press, 2004.

Cahn, Susan, *Coming on Strong: Gender and Sexuality in Twentieth-Century Women's Sport.* Cambridge MA: Harvard University Press, 1998.

Campbell, W. Joseph. "Not Likely Sent: The Remington-Heart 'Telegrams.'" *Journalism and Mass Communication Quarterly*, Summer 2000.

Chang, R. S., and J. M. Culp. "After Intersectionality." *University of Missouri–Kansas City Law Review* 71 (2002): 485–91.

Charlesworth-Seiler, Emma. "Stealing Home: Why Baseball Isn't America's National Pastime." Master's thesis, Department of Sociology, Hamline University, 2016.

Chomsky, Aviva, Barry Carr, and Pamela Smorkaloff. *The Cuba Reader: History, Culture, Politics.* Durham NC: Duke University Press, 2003.

Clodfelter, M. *Warfare and Armed Conflicts: A Statistical Encyclopedia of Casualty and Other Figures, 1492-2015,* 4th ed. Jefferson NC: McFarland, 2017.

Colorado Silver Bullets. http://www.coloradosilverbullets.org/.

Crenshaw, Kimberle Williams. "Mapping the Margins: Intersectionality, Identity Politics, and Violence against Women of Color." In *Public Nature of Private*

Violence, edited by Martha Albertson Fineman and Roxanne Mykitiuk, 93–118. New York: Routledge, 1994.

Cuadras, Pablo Antonio. *El Nicaragüense*. Managua: PINSA, 1971).

Doran, Terry, ed. *A Road Well Traveled: Three Generations of Cuban American Women*. Washington DC: Women's Educational Equity Act Program, United States Department of Education. 1988.

Echevarría, González. *The Pride of Havana: A History of Cuban Baseball*. New York: Oxford University Press, 1999.

Ewell, Judith. *The Human Tradition in Latin America: The Twentieth Century*. New York: Rowman and Littlefield, 1989.

Feminist Majority Foundation. *Empowering Women in Sports*. Empowering Women Series, no. 4. Arlington VA: Feminist Majority Foundation, 1995. feminist.org /research/sports/sports2.html.

Fidler, Merrie. "Baseball's Women on the Field during WWII." In *Who's on First: Replacement Players in World War II*, edited by Marc Z. Aaron and Bill Nowlin, with associated eds. James Forr and Len Levin, 374–89. Phoenix AZ: SABR, 2015.

———. "The Development and Decline of the All-American Girls Baseball League, 1943–1954." MS thesis, University of Massachusetts, Amherst, 1976.

———. *The Origins and History of the All-American Girls Professional Baseball League*. Jefferson NC: McFarland, 2006.

Fincher, Jack. "The 'Belles of the Game' Were a Hit with Their Fans." *Smithsonian* 20 (1999): 88–97.

Galt, Margot Fortunato. *Up to the Plate: The All American Girls Professional Baseball League*. Minneapolis: Lerner Publications, 1995.

Gilbert, Sarah. *A League of Their Own* (novelization of the feature film). New York: Warner Books, 1992.

Gottsman, Jane. *Game Face: What Does a Female Athlete Look Like?* New York: Random House, 2001.

Gregorich, Barbara. *Women at Play: The Story of Women in Baseball*. San Diego: Harcourt, Brace, 1993.

Hanmer, Trudy J. *The All-American Girls Professional Baseball League*. New York: New Discovery Books, 1994. American Events Series.

Helmer, Diana Star. *Belles of the Ball Park*. Brookfield CT: Millbrook Press, 1993.

Hensley, Beth H. "Older Women's Life Choices and Development after Playing Professional Baseball." EdD diss., University of Cincinnati, 1995.

Huff, Kristin. "A Personal Reflection on Women's Baseball." Unpublished manuscript. Author's personal collection, n.d.

Johnson, Susan E. *When Women Played Hardball*. Seattle: Seal Press, 1994.

Keenan, Jerry. *Encyclopedia of the Spanish-American & Philippine-American Wars*. Santa Barbara: ABC-CLIO, 2001.

Kovach, John. *Benders: Tales from South Bend's Baseball Past*. South Bend IN: Greenstocking Press, 1987.

Langley, Lester, *The Banana Wars: United States Intervention in the Caribbean, 1898–1934*. Chicago: Dorsey Press, 1988.

Lehman, Don, Jr. *Colonialism to Independence: Southeast Asia 1511–2014*. Morrisville NC: LuLu Press, 2015.

Litoff, Judy, and David Smith. *American Women in a World at War: Contemporary Accounts from World War II*. Lanham MD: Rowman and Littlefield, 1996.

Madden, W. C. *The All-American Girls Professional Baseball League Record Book: Comprehensive Hitting, Fielding and Pitching Statistics*. Jefferson NC: McFarland, 2000.

———. *The Hoosiers of Summer*. Indianapolis IN: Guild Press, 1994.

———. *The Women of the All-American Girls Professional Baseball League: A Biographical Dictionary*. Jefferson NC: McFarland, 1997.

Martí, José. *José Martí Reader: Writings on the Americas*. Edited by Ivan A. Schulman. London: Ocean Press, 2006.

Miller, Ernestine. *Making Her Mark: Firsts and Milestones in Women's Sports*. New York: McGraw-Hill, 2002.

Muench, Matthew. "More Girls Playing High School Baseball." ESPN. October 17, 2011. http://espn.go.com/blog/high-school/baseball/post/_/id/519/changing-the-game-girls-in-high-school-baseball.

Navarro, Jose Canton. *History of Cuba*. Havana: Si-Mar, 1998.

Osborne, Carol A., and Fiona Skillen. *Women in Sports History*. New York: Routledge, 2012.

Park, Roberta J., and Patricia Vertinsky. *Women, Sport, Society: Further Reflections, Reaffirming Mary Wollstonecraft*. New York: Routledge, 2011.

Perez, Louis, Jr. *Cuba: Between Reform and Revolution*. New York: Oxford University Press, 1995.

———. *Cuba in the American Imagination: Metaphor and the Imperial Ethos*. Chapel Hill: University of North Carolina Press, 2008.

———. *On Becoming Cuban: Identity, Nationality, and Culture*. Chapel Hill: University of North Carolina Press, 1999.

Pettavino, Paula, and Geralyn Pye. *Sport in Cuba: The Diamond in the Rough*. Pittsburgh: University of Pittsburgh Press, 1994.

Pfister, Gertrud, and Ilse Hartmann-Tews. *Sport and Women: Social Issues in International Perspective*. New York: Routledge, 2005.

Pierman, Carol J. "The All-American Girls Professional Baseball League: Accomplishing Great Things in a Dangerous World." In *Across the Diamond: Essays on Baseball and American Culture*, edited by Edward J. Rielly, 97–108. Binghamton NY: Haworth, 2003.

———. "Baseball, Conduct, and True Womanhood." *Women's Studies Quarterly* 33, no. 1/2 (Spring 2005): 60–85.

Pratt, Mary. *Preserving Our Legacy: A Peach of a Game*. Self-published, Quincy MA, 2004.

Purdy, Sam. "Revolutionary Béisbol: Political Appropriations of 'America's Game' in Pre- and Post-Revolution Nicaragua." *Yale Historical Review* 1, no. 2 (Spring 2010).

Ring, Jennifer. *A Game of Their Own: Voice of Contemporary Women in Baseball*. Lincoln: University of Nebraska Press, 2015.

Roepke, Sharon. *Diamond Gals: The Story of the All American Girls Professional Baseball League*. Marcellus MI: AAGPBL Cards 1986.

Sargent, Jim. "Earlene 'Beans' Risinger." http://oabi.org/bioproj/person/532b61cc. Accessed November 22, 2019.

———. *We Were the All Americans: Interviews with the Players of the AAGPBL, 1943–1954*. Jefferson NC: McFarland, 2013.

Scott, Joan. "Gender: A Useful Category of Historical Analysis." *American Historical Review* 91, no. 5 (1986): 1053–75.

Sexton, Maria. "Implications of the All-American Girls Baseball League for Physical Educators in the Guidance of Highly-Skilled Girls." Type C Project, Advanced School of Education, Teachers College, Columbia University, 1953.

Seymour, Harold. *Baseball: The People's Game*. New York: Oxford University Press, 1990.

Shattuck, Debbie. "Playing a Man's Game: Women in Baseball in the U.S." MS thesis, University of Colorado, Colorado Springs, 1993.

Smith, Lissa. *Nike Is a Goddess: The History of Women in Sports*. New York: Atlantic Monthly Press, 1999.

Stevenson, Rosemary, and W. C. Madden. *Don't Die on Third*. Monticello NY: Madden Enterprises, 2006.

Stoner, Kathryn Lynn. *From the House to the Streets: The Cuban Woman's Movement for Legal Reform, 1898–1940*. Durham NC: Duke University Press, 1991. Kindle edition.

Thomas, Hugh. *Cuba: The Pursuit of Freedom*. Boston: First Da Capo Press, 1998.

Thrombe, Carolyn. *Dottie Wiltse Collins*. Jefferson NC: McFarland, 2005.

Treadwell, Mattie. *The Women's Army Corps*. United States Army in World War II, Special Studies, 1954; reprint Washington DC: U. S. Army Center of Military

History, 1991. history.army.mil/books/wwii/wac/index.htm. Accessed December 15, 2015.

Tucker Institute for Research on Girls and Women in Sport, University of Minnesota. cehd.umn.edu/tuckercenter/research/default.html.

Vilaboy, Sergio Guerra. *Cuba: A History*. London: Ocean Press, 2010.

Women's Sports Foundation website. www.womenssportsfoundation.org/.

INDEX